GW01150626

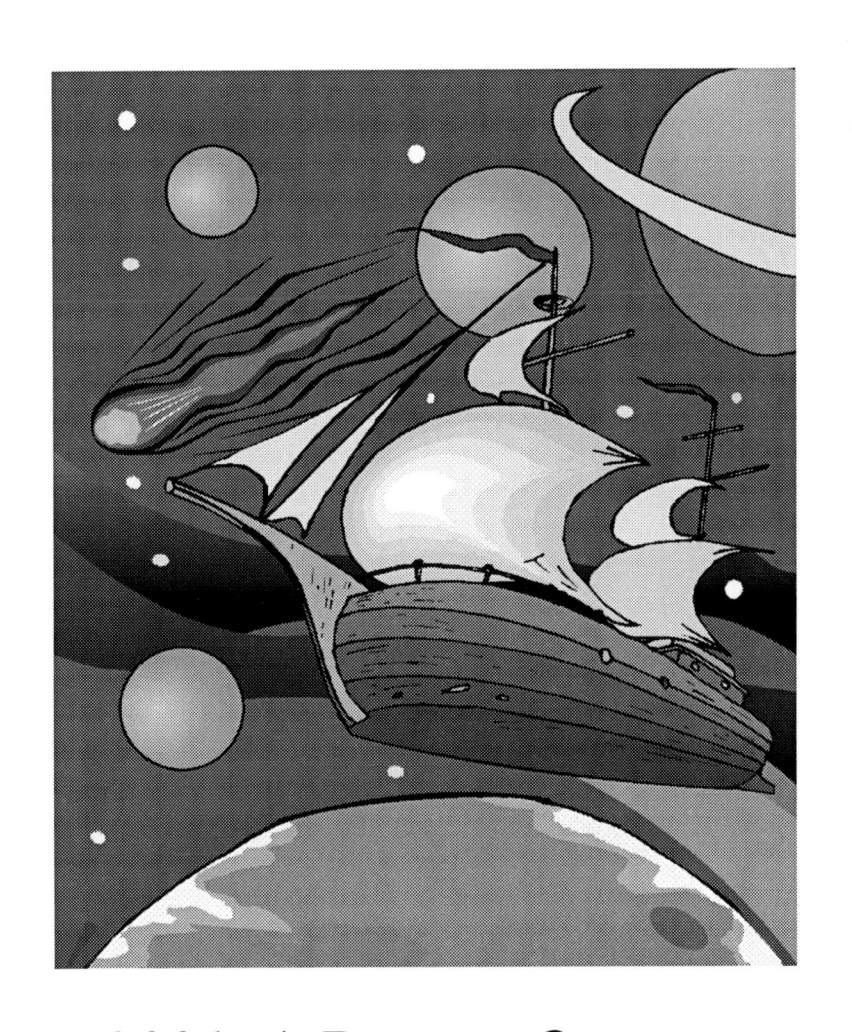

2001: A POETRY ODYSSEY SOUTH LONDON

Edited by Steve Twelvetree

First published in Great Britain in 2001 by
YOUNG WRITERS
Remus House,
Coltsfoot Drive,
Peterborough, PE2 9JX
Telephone (01733) 890066

All Rights Reserved

Copyright Contributors 2001

HB ISBN 0 75433 020 6
SB ISBN 0 75433 021 4

FOREWORD

Young Writers was established in 1991 with the aim to promote creative writing in children, to make reading and writing poetry fun.

This year the 2001: A Poetry Odyssey competition again proved to be a tremendous success with over 50,000 entries received nationwide.

The amount of hard work and effort put into each entry impressed us all, and is reflective of the teaching skills in schools today.

The task of selecting poems for publication was a difficult one but nevertheless, an enjoyable experience. We hope you are as pleased with the final selection in *2001: A Poetry Odyssey South London* as we are.

CONTENTS

Alleyn's School

Stefan Baker	1
Holly Allen Cooper	1
Polly Checkland Harding	2
Felix Le Vay	2
Tony Terroni	3
Hannah Tottenham	3
Panikos Oritis	4
Penny Lowe	4
Zuleika Salter	5
Gian-Filippo Scarpati	5
Alisha Meertins	6
Michael Edgar	7
Lydia Gabriel	8
Hannah Carnegy	8
Rebecca Bernard	9
Mia Neve	10
Alice Saville	11
Cate Luce	12
Digory Macfarlane	13
Lydia van den Bosch	14
Roman Subbotin	15
Harriet Piercy	16
Camilla Grundy	17
Harry Lewis	18
Araminta Markes	18
Freddie Besant	19
Grace Welch	20
Hayato Aida	21
Alice Cady	21
Sarah Douglas	22
Daisy Evans	22
Imogen Bland	23
George Savell	24
Nathaniel Bellio	24
Rachel Hunter	25

Fielder Camm	26
Charlotte Senior	26
Lizzy Frost	27
Gerard Mitchell	28
Orlando de Lange	29
Louise Morris	30
Robert Crowley	30
Jonny Rose	31
Toby Hoskins	32
Rusja Foster	32
Chloë Courtney	33
Emily Fletcher	34
Adam Fletcher	35
Danny Brewer	36
Alex Marshall	37
Rózsa Farkas	38

Bacon's College

Rebecca Samura	38
Jodie King	39
Chloe Townsend	39
Si Yan Long	40
Katey Adler	40
Daniel Hale	41
Laura Fitzgerald	41
Jessie Massey	42
Minh-nhi Dang	42
Jack Jenkins-Hill	43
Charley Baker	43
Stephen Seales	44
Andrea Asare	44
Gelle Dahir	45
Jake Lush	45
Aleisha Naomi Mehmet	46
Ashleigh Gosbee	46
Jayne Alice Douglas	47
Colette Brook	47
Deborah Kayode	48

	Ria Hopgood	48
	Ekemini Ekaneni	49
	Temi Adenugba	49
	Imranul Islam	50
	Samantha Shipman	50
	Emma Kelway	51
	Lucie Thorn	51
	Sam Guile	52
	Matthew Oryang	52
	Vanessa Agyemang	53
	Carly Hazell	53
	Kay Rozier	54
	Laura Jane Lennard	54
	Jenny Hodges	55
	Hok Shun	55
	Monique Ayton	56
	Franki Longman	57
	Jeffrey Tieku	57
	Melissa Stevens	58
	Gary Hole	58
	Tom Finch	58
	Damilola Lasisi Agiri	59
	Ian Richardson	59
	Hannah Abiola	60
	James Williams	61
	Christy Naish	61
	Blake Richardson	62
Bredinghurst School		
	Jermane James Ranson	62
	Tyrone Vidal	63
	Anton Jacques	63
	Lee Jarvis	64
Catford Girls School		
	Lauren Green	64
	Sharnell Marcelle	65
	Charlene Keyes	66

Chestnut Grove School
- Scott Mizzi — 66
- Ben Simpson — 67
- Jordan Edge — 67
- Helena Vidot — 68
- Galina Gorlova — 68
- Callum Campbell — 69
- Louis Wright — 69
- Reece Rose — 70
- Alexander Martin — 70
- Gemma Moram — 71
- Hollie Graham — 72
- Gemma Tester — 72
- Chantelle Mason — 73
- Kelly Plaine — 73
- Michael Delahaye — 74
- Shantelle Patricia Collins — 74
- Hülya Hassan & Camilla Evans — 75
- Courtney Ferlance — 75
- Natasha Patterson-Waugh — 76
- Nick East — 76
- Ruth N'Choh — 77
- James Armian — 78
- Paul Clayton — 79
- Roena Williams — 80
- Raymond Yuill — 81
- Gemma Currell — 82

Crofton School
- Victor Ohene — 82
- Samice Morris — 83
- Airam Myrie — 83
- Donna McVitie — 84
- Natasha Baptiste — 84
- Ricky Ryan — 85
- Jamiel Thomas — 86
- Lisa Holmes — 86
- Dariye Havutcu — 87

Eloise Dickie	87
Luther Alcide-Coghiel	88
Emma Tapley	88
Dean Constantinou	89
Hulya	89

Emanuel School

Zara Frith	90
Justin Moll	90
Marcus Aitman	91
Samantha Lewis-Purkis	91

Lycée Français Charles De Gaulle School

Guillaume Lincoln	92
Jessica White	92
Stephanie Foin	93
Natalia Boolaky	94
Alison Novic	95
Alexandra Michell	96
Corinne Smart	97
James Haydon	98
Alexander Maudhuit	99
Giannina Kline	100
Raphaël Rashid	101
Nathaniel Carter	102
Hugo Minchin	103
Claire Thompson	104
Hannah Creasey	105

Oak Lodge School

Karen Kelly	106
Clive Young	106
Jani Begum	107
Faheem Malik	108
Seon Anderson	108

Riverston School
Rebecca Penfold	109
Courtney Riley	109
Lianne Hemblade	110
Ashley Thanni	110
Oluwafemi Okulaja	111
Femi Sijuade	112
Gavin Shirley	112
Rolande Seudieu	113
James Thomas	114
Marialena Andreou	114
James Allen-Thompson	115
Maryanne Carlin	116
Simeon Brown	117
Henrietta Taylor	118
Victor Alaike	118
Michael Brooks	119
Bhavik Upadhyay	119
Natasha Clarke	120
Akinsola Akinbolagun	121

St Francis Xavier Sixth Form College
Seke Bangudu	122
Brenda Osieyo	123
Francessca Haffner	124
Tariro Masukume	125
'Revolt', Sacha Jason	126

Sydenham High School
Frances White	128
Lucy Kiernan	128
Theadora Foster	129
Angelique Forrester	129
Samantha Eniola Pereira	130
Natasha Mitchell	130
Aysem Hashim	131
Leila Sharif	131
Katie Mountain	132

Louisa McLellan	132
Charlotte Oram	133
Julia Charteris	134
Elizabeth Afolabi	134
Chloë McCarthy	135
Alice Lindsay	136
Elizabeth Lindsay	136
Beatrice Butler-Bowdon	137
Annie Broadbent	137
Nicola Graham	138
Duriyen Mehmet	138
Jemma Jackson	139
Rachel Harvey	140
Sheena Ganatra	141
Charlotte Head	142
Tana Forte	143
Annabel Head	144
Laura Jones	145
Sophie Hughes	146
Emma Louise Frempong-Manso	146
Devisha Patel	147
Agatha Knowles	148
Chloé Brown	148
Sarah Baumann	149
Katie Wardle	150
George Harrington	150
Claire Brockliss	151
Jennifer Lock	152
Fleur Nieddu	152
Seraphina Evans	153
Adelina Adjei	154
Harriet Bothwell	155
Hayley Hawkins	156

The Froebel School

Nathalie Clough	156
Gabby Laurent	157
Erika Bacon	158

Walworth School
- Jade Wick — 159
- Michael John — 160
- Emma-Jayne Maflin — 160
- Omotayo Kukuspecial — 161
- John Olanipekun — 162
- Sophie Morley — 162
- Nicola Hold — 163
- Morgan Schofield — 163
- Charlie Brightwell — 164
- Sarah Coote — 164
- Julia Sykes — 165
- Bukola Ogunjimi — 166
- Chelsea Kelly — 167

Westwood High School for Girls
- Susan Wain — 168
- Loredana Geoghegan — 168
- Nicole Iesi — 169
- Nikki Haman — 169
- Kylie Wood — 170
- Arooj Ahmed — 171
- Jodianne Griffiths — 172
- Fahmida Mossabbir — 172
- Anntoinette Ussher — 173
- Opal Plummer — 173
- Amy Heard — 174
- Hayat El-Daoud — 175
- Justine Bristow — 176
- Keisha Bristol — 176
- Adriana Crooks — 177
- Charlotte Nash — 177
- Claudine Parr — 178
- Jenny Demmen — 178
- Laura Mitchell — 179
- Maria Tough — 180
- Monique Baker — 180
- Simone Byer — 181

Jade Ashman	181
Sumayya Choudhury	182
Rhea Currie	182
Ameena Salik	183
Louise Johnson	183
Gemma Agard	184
Hannah Stevens	184
Elizabeth McAuslan	185
Joanne Machin	185
Tyenicha Hewitt	186
Josephine Osei-Nyarko	186
Terriejane Snell	187
Lucy Adams	188
Razia Jeerooburkhan	188
Natalie Parbodee	189
Kirsty Dowling	189
Sarah Benham	190
Michelle Scripps	190
Sara Widdowson	191
Farah Parekh	191
Kylie Evans	192
Tacy Ram	192
Charlotte Edwards	193
Hina Khwaja	193
Charlene Gogognon	194
Diana Monteiro	195
Emma McDowell	196
Shikiera Betts	196
Cherrowne McPherson	197
Nicole Ramsay	197
Aisha Abid	198
Jemma Haynes	198
Zainab Dawodu	199
Natalie Preen	199
Zeenat Malik	200
Michelle Wain	200
Niroshine Sureshkumar	201
Justine Tulloch	202

Justine Agbowu	202
Tina Bigley	203
Tenika Chin	203
Angela Hazell	204
Danielle Harris	204
Precious Ihuomah	205
Lauren Andrews	205
Laura Einecker	206
Sabrina Wholas	206
Ahzariaeha Harvey	207
Manisha Sharma	207
Vikki Heath	208
Tara Forde-Wildman	208
Louise Thompson	209
Crystal Lindsay	209
Fozia Haroon Karim	210
Kim Carter	210
Laura Panayides	211
Nicola Claridge	211
Tasneem Haroon Karim	212
Sophie Hassel	213
Sophie Rankin	214
Donna Stanley	214
Marium Bhatti	215
Mariam Mehdi	215
Christina Murray	216
Kelly Goff	216
Grace Coughlan	216
Pinar Mehmet	217
Natalie Papaspyrou	217
Marsha Francis	218
Sandy Lee	218
Atiqa Khan	218
Rachel Irwin	219
Kirsty Aboagye	219
Jane Sammut	220
Grace Mann	220

The Poems

THE PARK

The sun shines down through the clouds
The shade of the trees eclipse its mighty rays.
The treetops glimmer and the squirrels scavenge
Looking for food, walnuts, conkers and cherries.
Children play their games and relax in the shade
But I like looking at the sunny sky.
The sparkles of light help the flowers grow
Poppies, dandelions and rose bushes.
A breeze creeps up from the south
The sun makes its steady fall under the horizon
And then it goes down.
Badgers, hedgehogs and foxes come out to hunt
But I like looking at the starry sky.
The children retreat for their night-time rest.
The squirrels return to their treetop homes
But I like looking at the sparkling, starry sky.

Stefan Baker (11)
Alleyn's School

EUROPEAN FIELD

Overwhelming, but not threatening,
Inquisitive, watching. Silent.
So many companions,
But yet seem lonely.
Sad and questioning, looking for guidance.
So different, yet all the same.
They put life in perspective.
Each with their own personality,
Own expression.
Thirty-five thousand.

Holly Allen Cooper (13)
Alleyn's School

MY MAGIC BOX

Inside my magic box I have,
The songs of angels,
The beat of a butterfly's wing,
The fire of dragons,
The prance of a unicorn,
The feathers of a phoenix,
The fury of a bull,
The purr of a cat,
The roar of a lion.
All of these things are magical, wonderful
                                  beautiful things,
Kept in a very special place,
This place has battles
It has flowers,
And rivers and many other mysterious things,
It has a key,
Which only the owner can find
It is my brain.

Polly Checkland Harding (11)
Alleyn's School

IN THE SHADOW OF THE LIGHT

Beyond the flickering candle flame,
Something hidden out of sight,
In the shadow of the light.
For in a crowd I walk alone
Within my prison cell
Of flesh, blood and bone.
As I look up to see the stars
There in the shadow of the light
I remembered the brightness in the night.

Felix Le Vay (12)
Alleyn's School

THE BEAUTY OF NARCISSUS
(Based on a painting by Salvador Dali)

Beauty brings pain and hatred,
Beauty is nothing more than blood,
For the boy Narcissus in a world where his beauty shall crack.
He watches the egg so plain and dull,
But then it cracks and a flower a beautiful flower appears.
In a pool of endless time,
In a pool of endless beauty,
A wish that he could turn back that endless time,
When he saw that face as pretty as a flower,
Free and happy until,
His beauty was taken for granted,
This gift from the gods was crushed by the very same gods,
And so he grew older,
Day by day,
Hour by hour,
No time counts,
For the boy Narcissus stands here,
Here in the pool of sadness forever and a day.

Tony Terroni (12)
Alleyn's School

ALONE

Alone, I sit and stare
at the night sky
Vast and dark above me
Pricked by shining stars.
Wispy grey clouds float across
The pale moon.
Alone, I sit in the moonlight
Alone, by my window.

Hannah Tottenham (11)
Alleyn's School

THE MEXICAN MEN
*(The picture was painted by Pablo Picasso and was called
The Three Musicians)*

The Mexican men are here again
and playing their music is what they do best.

Tring goes the guitar!
Toot goes the clarinet!
As they watch the black and white notes run along.

The sweet music flies along down the street
whistling into people's ears.
Until!
The Mexican men are going home to make up a brand-new song.

Panikos Oritis (12)
Alleyn's School

FIRST CLASS PEACOCK

A lady in a carriage in a first class train,
Always needs a hat when she's in the rain.
'I must have this, I must have that,'
She says while perfecting the angle of her hat.

But . . .

Think through this, it isn't funny,
Look at her hat which cost all that money.
See the peacock feather on her head,
Does she spare a thought for the peacock that's

. . . dead?

Penny Lowe (12)
Alleyn's School

REFLECTIONS
*(A poem about the painting called
'Polishing Pans' by Marianne Stokes)*

Her delicate aching hand and grubby cloth circle the shining brass,
As the fine grey soot touches her face she grows greyer,
She works in silence,
All but the occasional faint squeak of the cloth rubbing the metal.
Hour by hour she scrubs the pan until at last,
Her bleak face stares back at her.
She is half asleep.
But the brightly gleaming metal keeps her awake.
She waits for the moment she can smell clean air,
Escape from this polluted room,
Are they clean enough?
Will she be punished if they aren't?
She stops, sighs, and continues her hard work of aching hands
                                          and shiny metal.

Zuleika Salter (12)
Alleyn's School

THE SURFER
(The painting was called The Great Wave by Katsushika Hakusui)

My destiny is in front of me;
it climbs higher and higher,
I approach it with anxiety as
its claws are eager to wrap me up.

As it comes down my reflex actions go to the right,
I have successfully accomplished my goal,
But I was not scared as I thrive on my vicious blue wave.

Gian-Filippo Scarpati (12)
Alleyn's School

FLIGHT OF ICARUS
*(Based on the picture: Flight Of Icarus
Painted by: Henri Matisse)*

He flies like a bird through the sunlit sky.
With no worries in the world,
Until he flies to the appealing sun.
His wax melts,
He plummets to the water.

Now he's in Heaven flying so elegantly through the sky.
Strolling through the clouds and past the stars,
Trying to find the magical key.
To unlock his secret love from the spell,
To stop him from having his heart broken once again.

As he moves higher and higher into the heavens,
The journey for the key gets harder and harder,
Ghosts and ghouls try to stop him
And his cousin who died tried to kill him,
But he knew no matter how clumsy he was, that he'd defeat them.

He carries on flying to the peak of the sky.
Past the ghosts, ghouls and his cousin.
Into the place where the angels are.
To help him save his loved one
And find the key.

She told him:
'Time is short my young boy,
your loved one's life is getting short.
The key you need is east from here,
fly away and do not fear.'

He flies east and finds the key
So starts his journey back to where his loved one is.
He's almost there but a tragedy occurs. He drops the key into oblivion.
He's angry and grieved because he killed his loved one,
And with his anger he swears and curses and is banished to Hell for life.

Alisha Meertins (12)
Alleyn's School

THE FALL

It is cold upstairs.
The strong, chilling wind blows out my third attempt
To light my filthy habit,
I fumble awkwardly with the lighter,
Squinting as my eyes catch a glare from the reflected sun,
But something else is reflected.
A flag?
No. A person, their cloak swinging in the wind.
But why so close to the edge?
My throat suddenly dries as the reality hits me.
They are going to jump.
My mind wants to try and stop him but my legs refuse,
My heart is loud, fast, painful,
I watch the last corner of the swaying cloak disappear over the edge.
The world seems to have gone silent.
Why? Why? Why? Echoes in my head.
I could have tried to stop the person but I didn't,
And now he shall never breathe again.
I have watched a life live and die in a matter of seconds.
I pull my sweaty hands to my face, dropping my fags.
From now on I shall respect life.

Michael Edgar (13)
Alleyn's School

A Summer Scene
(A poem about the painting called
'Summer' by Claude Monet)

She sits, relaxed but composed,
Her cornflower blue skirt spreads into the quivering grass.
A small smile is nestled on her face,
But as she looks down towards her book
A breeze floats past, powdering her skin,
But she does not feel it for she is mezmerised by her book,
The words painting a picture in her mind,
Nothing disturbs her,
Not even her daughter racing round,
Her bare feet rustling the grass,
But she falls, laughing out loud
And gazes up at the clear sky.
This is the power of summer.

Lydia Gabriel (12)
Alleyn's School

Stranded
(Painting: Christina's World
Artist: Andrew Wyeth)

There am I, hiding in the grass
But from whom?
From what
And why?
I am stranded, lost inside myself
And sanity seems so far away.
As the wind whistles in my ears
I give up hope
And wish that I could drown in the sea of grass.

Hannah Carnegy (13)
Alleyn's School

WOMAN IRONING
*(This poem is about a painting called
'Woman Ironing' called Edgar Degas)*

Can you see these tears that fall?
Or do you not want to care?
As I press harder on my husband's shirt,
I wonder what it would be like without anger and hurt!

I cannot say that these past few days of married life have been the best,
But I wouldn't say they've been the worst.
My husband and I are like the couple who once touched the sky,
But the clouds came,
And blackened our hearts.

'Iron my shirt!'
'I want something to eat!'
'Do the washing!'
These are the words that I always hear,
These are the times that I wish he would disappear!

He treats me like an animal in a cage,
Makes me do what he wants,
And then never letting me out,
He must think I'm a slave!

Can you see these tears that fall?
Or do you not want to care?
As I press harder on my husband's shirt,
I wonder when my knight in armour,
Will release a lonely maid!

Rebecca Bernard (12)
Alleyn's School

A Secret Of The Night

Descend deep into the dark, dark forest,
Through mud, thorns and ferns.
Creep through the eerie shadows
In the midst of night,
Then you shall see a magical creature take flight.

Normally quiet and still, sitting within a hollow,
His old, ruffled, white plume frayed and tattered
Within his head such wisdom
The cogs whirl and churn round and round,
Clicking, winding, spinning like a Ferris wheel.
His mind brewing like a cauldron ready to erupt.
Every second a new idea, better than the last.

Never would you suspect such a marvellous display,
From a bird that sits in an ancient, gnarled tree all day.
Who would surmise something so shy could reach for the sky?
Up he roars like a rocket to the moon,
Through stars he swoops.

Alert!

His wings out-stretched, sleek and neat for miles.
His eyes fixed like topaz, specks of fire.
His beak as gold as the sun.
His talons as sharp as swords.
Ready for the kill.
His beak clenched tight as he plummets down.
Seconds later, ascending with pride and a culinary treat,
Such an elegant bird of prey,

Such an amazing aerodynamic array,
Such a wise old fowl.

Yes!

*You have guessed the secret of the night.
The wise old owl!*

*Mia Neve (11)
Alleyn's School*

THE ARTIST'S ROOM
*(This poem is written about a painting called
'A Corner Of The Artist's Room')*

A shrine to the long-forgotten past,
Unaffected by the world outside,
Is the artist's room, where time stands still.
The playful sunlight throws gentle shadows
On the faded wall's soft shades
While waiting in vain for nightfall.
The ruffled flowers will never wilt,
Nor the old wicker chair crumble to dust.
This room that holds so many dreams,
Will never change.
A lacy umbrella and cardigan
Hang abandoned in a shady corner.
As a part of the enchantment,
They will never be claimed.
Never will the delicate curtains
Flutter in the breeze;
Never will soft footsteps ring out
On the polished floor.
In this room from forgotten dreams,
Nothing will ever change.

*Alice Saville (12)
Alleyn's School*

My Father The Hero

I sat in the dark corner humming to
myself to drown out the screams of pain.
I was the only spectator of the torture
of an innocent boy, my brother.
My ears bled from the sounds of his
merciful cries.
The taste of my salty teardrops made my
stomach churn.
I could smell the blood-painted walls
burning my nostrils.
His young helpless body was thrown around
the room like a puppet with no strings.
With my heartbeat thumping in my head
I yearned to curl up and fade away.
But the slaps, the thumps and the screams
made my body tingle.
I had rage but my rage was taken over by my fear.
My father, once a hero to me now appeared
a loathsome coward.
My brother lay helpless and bruised on
the floor.
I did nothing as I knew it was my
turn next.

Cate Luce (13)
Alleyn's School

NIGHTHAWKS

It was a cold night in New York City.
The warm amber light from Fred's Bar drew me closer,
I had a drink and left the bar,
The dim neon sign flickering like a struggling firefly
Tormenting the frozen shadows.
I walked past the yawning black alleys and derelict warehouses
Following the chill of my breath.
A sharp scream pierced the silence,
I did not turn around,
I heard another voice shouting over the scream,
I froze.
Two shots.
The bullets echoed through the air,
The sound diminished,
The chamber was empty.
The air was full of the charred gunpowder.
Two beads of sweat fell from my brow,
I heard a man's voice mumbling,
The mumbling coming closer,
My heart beating faster,
I closed my eyes,
I prayed.
But still I could not move on that cold night in New York City
And then the footsteps stopped behind me . . .
I opened my eyes
And walked through the shadows in silence.
I woke up on that warm morning in New York City.

Digory Macfarlane (14)
Alleyn's School

DARK ALLEY

Late
Dark alley
No moon,
No escape.
Stomach churning,
Heart racing,
He's chasing me.
He has a knife,
I smell fear,
I taste sweat.
I hear the rush of footsteps on the cobbled pavement.
He's closing me down.
I'm clinging to my bag.
I feel his hot breath on my neck.
I feel a swipe across my back.
He's cut my bag from my shoulder.
I'm clinging on.
Squawk!
I turn to face him.
Frightened eyes,
Legs like jelly - I collapse.
Mouth dry,
White with fear and shaking.
he's standing over me,
His hands round my throat.
He's taken my bag.
His grip tightens,
I feel myself turning red.
Life is being stripped from me,
It's going, it's going, it's gone!

Lydia van den Bosch (13)
Alleyn's School

THE THREE MUSICIANS

There's us three:
Carlos, Fernando and me.
Here we are surrounded by a crowd,
Extremely loud.
But once we start playing
Everyone goes quiet,
Listen to music, for that they're paying,
And everyone is pleased by it.
Carlos on flute,
Me on guitar,
Fernando on xylophone:
Our music is tying us up like a knot.
And then the first coin rings,
Going into the pot.
And then there goes another hundred of them,
That's quite a lot!
So there I am in my yellow suit,
Carlos in white and blue, playing his flute.
And there's Fernando in black.
I'm surrounded in caramel colour:
Shadows in brown,
People are brown,
Everything's brown!
Now our tune has ended,
The crowd's gone wild and loud again.
They're busily talking to each other,
While we look at our gain.
There am I in a caramel world,
Where no one gets bored,
There's us three:
Carlos, Fernando and me.

Roman Subbotin (12)
Alleyn's School

THE PUNCHBAG

Here I crouch again - back underneath the kitchen table.
He can't reach me here, I'm safe from his fist,
Once again I hug my legs in tight against my body,
Resting my chin on my knee and closing my eyes.
I know those same angry shouts . . . the same stench of
                                  alcohol upon his breath.
I hear her cries for help as he beats her, smack after smack across
                                            her face.
I feel myself tremble from head to toe as she does,
I hear them as she's pushed about the room,
I feel her body giving a meek shudder of pain as she slides down the
wall on to the cold, hard floor hysterically.
I open my eyes slowly and look about myself intently . . . listening,
                                    watching . . . waiting . . .
The sun's rays shine through our small window at the top
                                  of the staircase.
The light warms the back of my head.
The peace is broken by her desperate whisper of mercy and hand
                                  clenched over the tablecloth . . .
I hear a sickening thud, . . . then nothing more
As the pungent stench of fresh blood seeps through the room like
                                  a disease,
I feel a tear trickle silently down my face.
I taste the salt upon my lips and I take one small spy through the
split in the tablecloth . . .
But he has seen me . . .

Harriet Piercy (13)
Alleyn's School

CORNFIELD QUESTIONS?

Winds rushing through large expanse of corn,
The small whimper of a lonely field mouse.
A shout from a mistress who is in the barn,
At last Christina has found the clue to life.
Essence of life,
But what is life?
For years upon years, she has been left without a playmate.
To enjoy this vast luxury that all children would love to endure.
Even without the sight of her small, pale face,
We can sense the soundless pools of tears streaming down her cheeks.
Never has she felt part of her family
She has spent her life being the odd one out.
She is the string to be about to be cut from the ball of wool,
Trying to remain part of what she knows so well.
A decision has been made.
Up she gets amongst the golden corn swaying in the fierce wind.
Trying to block out the butterflies that seem to be so excited.
The yellow highlights in her brown hair seem to reflect the colour
                                                        of the sun.
She keeps walking.
Past the stony bricks, and the rusty gate up to the front door.
She knocks timidly on the door and an echo floods through the house.
The small patter of the border collie's feet makes the girl feel as though a space that has been in her heart for a long time, has suddenly been filled.
The door opens and at once Christina is embraced by her mother.
Now she feels part of the jigsaw,
At home.

Camilla Grundy (12)
Alleyn's School

THE GARDEN OF GOOD AND EVIL
*(This poem is about a painting called
'Metamorphosis Of Narcissus' by Salvador Dali)*

There he stood not knowing where he was,
And there ahead he sees a golden hand,
With a giant glowing walnut at its finger tips.
There he looks to his right and notices a grey stone hand,
Holding a white egg where is born a frail flower.
They are the hands of good and evil,
Who choose where dead ones are placed.
Next to them is a peaceful pond,
The reflection of the golden hand is beautiful,
But the grey hand is nowhere to be seen.
There are stormy clouds on one side,
And lovely blue skies on the other.
What is this place? He thinks,
Is it heaven, hell, where am I?
Suddenly behind him appear people singing and dancing.
In the opposite direction a wolf devours a piece of rotting meat.

This is the garden of good and evil.

Harry Lewis (12)
Alleyn's School

THE NIGHT CRIME

The midnight bells go
In the long narrow street
I hear a scream, I run to and fro
I look up and see a man cutting meat.

I turn round and notice a shadow
I start running the opposite way
I look back; it's now gone low
I run faster and faster, I trip, I fall, I lay.

I hear footsteps coming
I felt someone grabbing me
I touch his face and open my eyes
I see a dark, tall man holding me.

'Your money or your life?' he shouts
'Here take my money.' I say in tears of fear.
He runs off, the thieving lout
I get up in anger and scream, 'Don't come near!'

Araminta Markes (13)
Alleyn's School

ESCAPE
*(This poem is about a painting called
'Christina's World' by Andrew Wyeth)*

As the girl lies down to rest,
She sinks into a dream,
She tries to get away from her life,
From the dreary farm chores,
She hates her farm in a vast expanse of nothingness,
And as she lies she feels as though she is the only one on this earth,
And the only one who cares,

She goes to lie in the cornfield,
She takes a last look at the farm and turns away,
She looks beyond the fields and valleys,
To a place far away,
Where people haven't gone,
Where she will go, someday,
But for now she will have to make do
With her world.

Freddie Besant (13)
Alleyn's School

The Cat

It slinks along the wall at night,
Winning each and every fight,
Its slick back hair,
Its wide eyes stare,
It scares every child,
People say its wild,
It's all old ladies talk about,
The cat, the cat, the cat
Some leave out food for the cat to eat,
The food disappears, but the cat they do not meet,
It's sly, it's cunning,
Its glossy coat is stunning,
It still climbs along the wall at night,
Still winning each and every fight,
The truth about the cat will never be found,
Because the cat makes no sound.

Grace Welch (11)
Alleyn's School

Captive Flesh

(This poem is about a painting called
'Captive Flesh' by William Hogarth)

The cat is in the background,
Looking at his flesh,
Trying to pounce at any,
To eat it up in his mouth.

But what is it waiting for?
The children are busy,
Not noticing what the cat is doing.

Perhaps the cat is thinking,
How to open the cage,
Without anyone noticing.

The cat's eye is gleaming,
On the panicking bird,
Will the cat ever catch it?
Would it be in his claws?

But just then,
The boy looks around at the bird,
Then, suddenly the cat pounced on the cage.

Hayato Aida (13)
Alleyn's School

MISS CICELY ALEXANDER
*(A poem about a painting
by James Abbott McNeill Whistler)*

There she stands all alone
Her beautiful face perfect
The lace she wears reflects the moon
Or is she glowing?
Her delicate pose makes her look more beautiful
But what is she looking at?
Her gaze is fixed beyond the camera lens
The hills in the background?
For they are truly beautiful
The stars in the ebony sky?
They shine so brightly
The flowing river?
So strong and bold
The lush vegetation?
No,
She is gazing at the mirror her mother holds
For she
Is the most beautiful.

Alice Cady (12)
Alleyn's School

I AM
*(A Poem about the painting called
'Big Women's Talk' by Sonia Boyce)*

I am different
I am unhappy
I am waiting

I am dreaming of the day when they accept me

I am crying
I am hurt
I am wasted

I am fed up with being told I will amount to nothing

I am stupid
I am foolish
I am an outcast

I am nothing so everybody tells me

I am hurt
I am right
They are wrong

My mother tells me that eventually the pain will pass me by.

Sarah Douglas (12)
Alleyn's School

THE BALLET DANCER

She is a ballet dancer
prancing round and round
like an agile pussy cat
pouncing on the ground
maybe a swooping bird
that never will be seen
and never even heard.

This ballet dancer is lucky
she is one of the chosen few
she has more dancing talent
than either me or you
she flies across the stage
like a bird in the sky
or your eyes across a page
for she is the ballet dancer
the most wonderful of all.

Daisy Evans (12)
Alleyn's School

INSIDE OUT

The mud is thick and so the gas,
They have us captured in their wrath.

The wind whistling the poppies on,
The larks, the trees, sing their song.

My breath becoming more and more scarce,
My chest burning, nothing compares.

Birds fly by like stones to throw,
The wind blowing rushes to and fro.

My world starts spinning round and round,
Feeling faint, I hit the ground.

Mice scrambling every which way to hide,
Now they nestle side by side.

My throat barricaded,
My lungs screaming out for air,
The showers are still going,
I lie helplessly bare.

Imogen Bland (12)
Alleyn's School

CREATURES WHY ARE THEY LIKE THIS?

The giraffes reach up high into the
tree-tops to get the luscious leaves in the trees.
Why are they like this?

The alligators swim through the
murky water snapping at any living thing.
Why are they like this?

The phoenix circles in the blue sky
a red fireball flying around.
Why is it like this?

Nobody knows!

George Savell (11)
Alleyn's School

AN ISOLATED CHILD

There hangs a picture, on the wall,
of a quiet girl, who longs to be tall.
With caring eyes, and brown short hair,
lips so red, and a face so fair.
Between her grubby fingers, sits a tiny turtle dove,
the way that she embraces it, shows only one thing, love.
On her simple dress, sits a knitted handkerchief,
made and shaped sublimely, just like an autumn leaf.
On the father's name in writing, she wrote that on the wall.

Nathaniel Bellio (13)
Alleyn's School

I AM THE CRIMINAL

I am the criminal,
I feel like the victim,
crouched in this corner,
awaiting escape.

I am the criminal,
hidden by darkness,
blood-drenched blade clutched
in my hot, trembling hand.

I am the criminal.
Do I hear voices?
Do I hear footsteps?
Or simply the sound of the pound of my heart?

I am the criminal,
the stench of the body
brushed away suddenly
by an icy-cold wind.

I am the criminal,
salty sweat pours
from my brow all the way
to my desert-dry throat.

I am the criminal,
murder, the crime,
sitting here waiting
until I get caught.

Rachel Hunter (13)
Alleyn's School

WAR OF THE WORLD, DEATH AND DEPRESSION

Guns pause as men run up from the ranks
Machine guns blaze cutting down the flanks

Men rush from the trenches
Laid to rest on the barbed wire fences

A gas bomb lands, a direct hit
Masks are placed but they won't fit

Crosses are given to the men that tried
Graves are given to the men that died

Many who went never came back
Given a gun but never got the knack

Planes are flown, shells are dropped
Officers think that the war has stopped

Women take over from the men that have gone
Not knowing how long the war will go on.

The rest is up to the books to tell
I wouldn't like it, probably like hell.

Fielder Camm (13)
Alleyn's School

A BED OF ROSES

From her sheltered room,
Into the midnight garden she tread.
Onto the frosty lawns,
From her white deathly bed.

Silhouette against the moon,
Pearl drop tear in eye.
Silver lips of pure ice,
Came as she did lie.

On her bed of roses,
On her bed of stone.
Arms folded against her chest,
There as she mourned alone.

Charlotte Senior (12)
Alleyn's School

CLARINET EXAM

I walk into the cold dark room.
Fear rushing from head to toe.
There's no going back now.

I smile at the two glaring eyes,
In the corner of the room.
It gives an evil grin back.
Then it speaks . . .

Dominant seventh,
In the key of B flat . . . tongued.
I laugh inside,
It can't catch me out this easily.
I play it perfectly.

I see the anger in its eyes.
Then it spoke again . . .
E flat minor melodic scale slurred.
The tone in its voice, was as if to say
Ha ha . . . I've got you this time.
But it hadn't.

I walk out of the cold dark room.
Happiness running from head to toe.
There's no going back in now.

Lizzy Frost (12)
Alleyn's School

THE SHADOW

The night was cold
and the moon was bright

The house was empty
all darkness, no light

The door creaked open
and in crept the shadow

He pulled out his gun,
so small, slim and narrow

He aimed it at Tommy
as he slept in the chair

Then Tommy woke up
and shouted 'Who's there?'

But the shadow squeezed the trigger
and the bullet screamed out

It hit Tommy's temple
and Tommy hit the ground

He stood over Tommy
all bloody and wrecked
just another victim,
just another one dead.

Gerard Mitchell (14)
Alleyn's School

BIG GAME, BIG LIE

Recruitment posters sing of it
fight the fight shall we

As a game is how he thinks of it
the air, the land, the sea

The air in the truck reeks of it
For mercy losers plee

His machine gun barrel is used in it
Shoot them, they and he

Death and hurt come of it
No fun and laughs of glee

Soon he is in the midst of it
A shot, a hit, a groan

A shot and he's almost killed in it
He cries as he wails and moans

You cannot make a joke of it
The blood, the death, the bone

Soon he'll have enough of it
And be galloping off to home

But he knows he can't be rid of it
All his fears are shown.

Orlando de Lange (12)
Alleyn's School

E'TAPLES

The plain prim white graves stand out amongst lush green grass,
But no flowers,
Swaying trees engulf the area,
And the wind rustles their leaves.
The tranquillity urges a prayer.
An unknown family's forgotten memories torment my mind.
A sea of graves envelope me,
As I wander through the past
The straight lines of graves stand to attention
Like the soldiers they resemble.
Neat barren flower beds are placed before graves.
The same white stone used over again
For pathways, entrances and monuments.
No clue of which grave to grieve at.
The stony grey sky reflects my mood and tries to outlive my emotions.
A multi-cultural graveyard where thousands were buried.

Louise Morris (11)
Alleyn's School

BREAKING WRISTS AND THE LAW

One day as I was walking home from school,
I turned down a side street,
What a sight,
Two large boys hitting a smaller boy.
I did what any good citizen would do,
I went to help the smaller boy.
As I ran down the street at lightning speed,
I charged one of the boys with my shoulder,
He went crashing to the ground.

Of course a fight ensued,
I fought them off but got a very hard blow,
With a stick across my forearm and suffered a broken wrist.

I didn't think much of it at the time,
I just helped the smaller boy up.

That all happened just a week ago,
When I was just sixteen,
Now on my seventeenth birthday,
As I write this I nurse a broken wrist
And all for being a good citizen.

Robert Crowley (13)
Alleyn's School

JACK

The clock struck twelve
The moon milky-white
An insignificant
Walked towards the lamp light
On that same road
A woman walked
Rich and proper
But her face pale and taut
The insignificant smiled
This woman would be easy
All he had to do was stab her twice
And she'd be dead and queasy
The woman looked up and saw a figure in the lamp
A queer man with a knife
She didn't have time to run or scream
As she was quickly robbed of her life
The distant clock struck 1am
The moon now obscured by mist
Jack scoured the deserted street
To see if there was a woman he'd missed.

Jonny Rose (13)
Alleyn's School

THE TILE

People go up and down the escalators,
running to catch their trains,
I see this and much more,
for I am a little tile on a wall,
when I look around I see millions of other tiles,
but none as nice as me,
I am not just an ordinary tile,
I am different from all those other tiles,
a young girl runs past,
and drops a small make-up mirror,
I see myself reflected,
I am after all just a little white tile,
just like all the other thousand that surround me,
a cold wind rushes through the tunnels,
for the station has long been deserted,
and all the tiles around me begin to drop off and smash,
I know my days are limited for soon I will fall,
and become no more than a pile of dirt and dust.

Toby Hoskins (11)
Alleyn's School

THE PEARL NECKLACE

The woman holds the necklace,
It shimmers like a chandelier.

The cat plays with it,
Showing its white chest,
Its white paws,
The rest of it black.

The woman's eyes are watching,
Closely, without fear.
She loves the cat, the necklace,
For they belong to her.

Rusja Foster (12)
Alleyn's School

HIM

When you look at him, what do you see?
The dark brown skin,
Rough like bark from years of toil.
The eyes, the penetrating eyes,
Like pools of stagnant water.
The long, lank hair,
Black, like a coiled rope of midnight.
The deep scars,
Etched like blood red rivers.
Is that all you see?

Or do you see . . .
A slave by his skin,
Just like any other?

Look deeper then.
Not a slave by the colour of his skin, never.

When I look at him I see . . .
A fierce soul,
Burning like fire.
That's what I see.

He's a diamond in the dust.

Chloë Courtney (11)
Alleyn's School

THE CAT

A slinky figure,
Moving through the shadows.
Graceful, but aware,
Aware of danger.

A hiss and a spit
Is all it needs to
Scare away anything
Bothering her.

And a flick of the tail,
And a lick of her paw
And maybe a purr
Shows us who's the boss,

She moves elegantly,
But not like a coward,
For we know she can manage
Without a blink.

She can be more,
Than just a cat.
More like a tiger
Some would say.

For she rules the area
Everyone knows that,
No one will contradict her,
No one at all.

Emily Fletcher (11)
Alleyn's School

THE ANIMAL RACE

If all the animals in the world,
Every colour, every face,
Gathered together under one roof,
To take part in an animal race.

'The cheetah now is in the lead,
Shocking the crowd with its lightning speed,
Then, allowing its fans to blink,
The cheetah stops! It needs a drink.

Then up in front, here comes the sparrow,
His wingspan great, his body narrow,
But then with an almighty scream,
The sparrow stops! It's out of steam.

Now up in front will come the skunk,
Producing its disgusting funk,
But then it's hit a little mound,
What's left of the skunk thing on the ground.

Then all together like a flash,
There is a most earth-shattering crash,
And with a time of 90:10,
The tortoise wins it yet again.

And next year it'll be the same,
All the glory, all the fame.

So many things he has achieved,
So many that it's not believed,
It drives that hare right round the bend,
The winnings of our green, shelled friend.'

Adam Fletcher (11)
Alleyn's School

LEAVING A WORLD BEHIND

Whoa! There goes the world again as I seemingly rise out into nowhere,
The white walls of a box engulf my brain into overload,
I cannot think,
The green goodness is all I have to satisfy myself in these alien
                                                          surroundings,
   The floor vibrates and I feel it surging,
   The hot sun on my face,
The tingle of the green grass below me,
Faces block out the warmth and shine as my little nest disappears,
I'm introduced to a whole new world so quickly,
I was taken out of an old house and put into a new,
As darkness descends the shadows start to attack me,
My only intention is to live the night through,
White-tailed creatures whip through the night,
Long, thin and fast as they leap over the boundaries,
The places I have not explored, they have,
The adventures I hope to achieve they don't even have to try,
They approach with caution,
Every step that they take makes neither noise nor sound,
They get ready to pounce onto what is at the moment my hiding place
                                                          and my home,
I get to flinch when quicker than a crack of a whip they're gone,
As the door shuts with a bang I'm safe,
Until next time.

Danny Brewer (11)
Alleyn's School

THE CAT

He crouches in the long green grass
Stalking coloured butterflies,
Not one of them will he let pass
Territory behind him lies.

He prowls around the garden walling,
Leaping nimbly, fence to fence,
A tightrope walker, never falling
His eyes are sharp, his muscles tense.

Tiger markings on his fur
Blend him with the autumn leaves
His figure is a shapeless blur,
As he darts between the trees.

As the setting sun sinks low
And darkness impregnates the blue
The twilight has a pinky glow
The day is old, the night is new.

He saunters home to drink and eat
Towards the hearth rug he well knows,
And cosily begins to sleep
While the warm fire softly glows.

Alex Marshall (11)
Alleyn's School

THE TRENCHES

Writhing bodies look up and gasp.
People around me are falling fast.
My hands grow cold, I seize to tell.
My heart beats faster, I think I fell.
These green clouds are, suffocating fast.
Gas helmet on, it is my mask
I smile grimly, take a glance
I think it may just be my last.
Why not take a look? I think
But my eyes won't open. Not to blink.
These patches of poppies, they do seem
To mix in with bloodshot wound on green.
Screams, shouts and beacons call,
They call to make a human wall.
My eyes are weeping
I cannot see
Please! Please! Release me!

Rózsa Farkas (12)
Alleyn's School

THE WAVE

The wave was crashing and storming
as it roared past me,
it was like a monster
trying to get me.

The spray of the waves reminds
me of a cold shower,
something whistles but there's
nobody around.
Wait, it's just the sea.

Rebecca Samura (11)
Bacon's College

THE POEM OF THE DEEP!

The deep blue sea
The deep blue sea
Splashing all over me
I'm sailing away, rocking side by side
With the lighthouse light leading my guide
The moon is shining onto the sea
With the fishes swimming, swimming free
I'm nearly there, there onto the shore.
With the sand spread around the floor,
The deep blue sea
The deep blue sea
Splashing all over me.

Jodie King (11)
Bacon's College

THE WAVE

The wave was a giant hand,
Reaching out to get me.
The wave sounded like . . .
. . . a giant roaring.

It was falling over me,
Soon it would be in the water again.
I could feel the spray from the wave,
I felt like I was in a shower.

The wave was reaching high,
As high as the sky.
Will it crash down,
No . . . it will not.

Chloe Townsend (11)
Bacon's College

THE CHAMELEON CLAWS

The waves are claws,
small chameleon claws,
trying to grab the canoes.
While the claws are grabbing it
scratches,
cat stratches,
reveals a death to all.
They return from the deep blue sea,
but to our horror
pebbled like snow and rain drops down on you and me.
But suddenly a sunny day saves us,
As if it's a great ball of fire.
The claws and pebbles will never be seen
by those who live in that awful scene.

Si Yan Long (11)
Bacon's College

THE HAND

The wet, dripping hand, reached out and sang:
tomorrow will be a lonely day,
the clouds will hang low,
the sea will rage in temper,
so I suggest you stay at home.

The day after that will be as
sunny as your smile,
so why don't you come out,
just for a little while . . .

Then disappeared.

Katey Adler (11)
Bacon's College

THE SEA STORM

The sea, it was a hand,
A hand grasping the canon of the vessel,
Pulling us down into the mouth of the sea
And to the dark dingy depths of the ocean.
The front cabin light dimmed and flickered
With the water-logged electrics.
The engine failing with the watery petrol,
The ship was creaking with the weight of the sea around it.
The best the soldiers could do was sit and wait
While the huge metal monstrosity of a ship disintegrated around them.
They all knew that this was the time to get into the life boat and leave.
But there was only one small life boat!
It was like nothing you had ever seen before,
Hundreds of people punching, kicking and shooting.
This lasted one hour
And when it was over there was hardly anything left of the ship,
There were seven left and time was falling like an avalanche.
They scrambled into the boat and sailed away towards a hopeful light.

Daniel Hale (11)
Bacon's College

THE SEA WORLD

The wave was a sea monster coming towards my boat,
The colours of the sea went from white to black to grey,
The spray looks like icicles crushing as the wave fell down,
The hands were scraping the end of my boat,
The people began to beg to get to the edge of the mountain,
The wave was like a world on top of me,
The bottom of the boat was a devil beneath me
The bottom of the boat was a devil beneath me.

Laura Fitzgerald (11)
Bacon's College

THE EVENING ON THE ROCKY SEA!

The wave was a crocodile's claw grasping towards me.
It was so angry I was terrified.
The surface of the sea was very rough,
As the wave came upon me!
It became louder the closer I got
The wave clashing together made spray fling into my eyes!
We were nearly there.
Seaweed and water overflowing on board
Although knowing it was the storm and sea
It didn't take my mind off of it.

Jessie Massey (11)
Bacon's College

UNTITLED

Remember me when I am gone,
When you can no longer hold my hand,
But cry and hurt.
Remember me as I was,
Whom you knew and cared,
Not as me now, whom you should forget.
Remember me when you are sad,
For you should forget your troubles and smile.
Just remember me when I am no more
Day by day,
Yet if you should forget me for a while
And afterwards remember me,
Do not grieve,
For a wave of happy memories that
We forever share will replace your sorrow.

Minh-nhi Dang (14)
Bacon's College

UNTITLED

Huge waves hit the surface
They were a cold hearted teacher's hand
Cracking down on the table as she screamed.
The working men cried their prayers
They were ants
When you have just taken their bread roll away
The waves were undiscovered dinosaurs
With dribble coming from his mouth
And glaring cats eyes and sparkling ivory claws
The waves were in almost full camouflage
It was just the shape that gave him away.

Jack Jenkins-Hill (11)
Bacon's College

THE CHASE

My heart was racing like a bell,
It all felt like a visit to hell.

I had never felt so scared in my life,
It felt like being stabbed with a knife.

As thoughts raced through my head,
I felt and knew I was close to death.

'Take me back to 1999,
Quickly now, we're running out of time!'

I said these words as the clocks were ticking,
Concentrating, sweat was dripping.

Finally I'm home at last,
I'll never again try to mess with the past.

Charley Baker (11)
Bacon's College

HAND OF THE SEA

The vicious sea swayed, and curled
Crashed and bashed upon their opponents
Like a tiger tearing apart its prey.

The tumbling hand of the sea released danger
As boats paid the price
And were left isolated
Upon the once calm and loving sea

Time softly floated by
As lonely people began to cry
The lonely sky began to get dimmer
And the reign of the sea had just taken over.

Lives were at stake
And soon to be perished
Ones who lived
Will remember the night when the sea came alive.

Stephen Seales (11)
Bacon's College

THE SEA

The sea looked like a vicious fist,
eager to grab the boats,
the people in the boats screamed,
but the vicious fist grabbed the boats,
and threw it over to the other side of the sea
the vicious fist disappeared and was never to be seen again.

Andrea Asare (11)
Bacon's College

VOICE OF THE SHARK MAN

I'm different from others
I feel isolated
I don't want to kill
but I can't stop killing.
I follow them to the beach
I see them going into the water
I try to stop myself
my heart says 'No'
but my brain and stomach say 'Yes'
I have no choice
but to eat.

I swim closer to them in my human form.
I feel my legs turning to fins,
I feel my body change to grey.
I feel the shark head going over my human head.
It's too late,
I can't stop myself.

Gelle Dahir (11)
Bacon's College

THE WAVE STORM

The waves were like claws
coming down on the people
taking the people under the water.
The waves were towering down on the men,
by now it looked like the waves were eating them.
The holes in the waves looked like big eyes,
the waves looked like monsters.

Jake Lush (11)
Bacon's College

FEAR POEM

As I lay there
On my bed, I
try to think of
something nice.
But all I can see
is this big black
hole waiting for
me to drop inside.
I feel scared,
my fingers are shaking,
what do I do?
I feel like there is
a whirlpool
going around my
head, with space
rockets going past,
as I lay there in
my bed.

Aleisha Naomi Mehmet (12)
Bacon's College

THE WAVES

The waves are mighty high
reaching for the sky.
The waves are pushing with all their might
trying to splash everything in sight.
The foam is like wavy hair
wanting to be combed
that's wishing it wasn't there.

Ashleigh Gosbee (12)
Bacon's College

THE LAST BREATH

The waves are hungry
The waves are strong
The boats are tough
But not tough enough.

The people are scared
The people are crying
The land is too far
And the sea is too fierce.

The boat is falling apart
The boats are going down
The people are falling
There's no land in sight.

The sea is still
The sea is bare
The sea is empty
The sea is dead.

Jayne Alice Douglas (11)
Bacon's College

THE SEA!

During the night the waves sway in a quick motion.
The falling waves' hands pushed themselves down to grab me.
As the waves pulled each other down to the bottom,
They clashed with the falling rocks.
My boat was swayed all over the place,
I couldn't realise where I was!
The mountain was a paused wave.
I am devastated by what happened,
Although I know it was the sea!

Colette Brook (11)
Bacon's College

MY EXPERIENCE

I could hear the waves,
Crashing, smashing and bashing into the boat,
The shouts of
Cries and sighs which surrounded me
And still I could not help them.
The power of the waves pulled us in
like a *black hole*
As I held on for life another person lost theirs
People shouted to me for help but
I had to bow my head in
Shame and guilt
I wished I did not survive now.
I am filled with pain for the rest of my life.
It was me!

Deborah Kayode (12)
Bacon's College

THE WAVE

It was a murky day.
The sea was tossing and turning.
There were hands on the edge of
each wave
diving down to get me.
The horses' legs were ready to stamp
on me.
I screamed and screamed but no one
answered me.
I prayed to God
let this end, let this end.

Ria Hopgood (11)
Bacon's College

THE POEM OF THE WAVE

Japanese drew this picture,
But didn't draw it during their lecture.
They drew a wave that looked like a hand,
That when the boats were coming they had to expand.
At the background of this picture,
You could see a mountain,
I don't know why it's here,
But I think it keeps the river flowing.
The river never stops doing its job,
But one day I think it'll do a plop.
They did a symbol on the picture that I don't understand,
But I think that they will have to change it
So they could understand.
The boat is moving about to tip,
But it can't tip, it'll have to do a flip.

Ekemini Ekaneni (11)
Bacon's College

MYSELF

Words used to describe me
Patient and calm
I really don't like things
That bring me any harm
I'm not that good
Not that bad
Having two brothers
Sometimes drives me mad!

Temi Adenugba (14)
Bacon's College

REPLY TO SHANI'S INSULTING POEM

Sorry!
But all you girls do is watch soaps, dramas and
Play with Barbie and Ken in their caravan as much as you
Can, all which is really boring,
From a boys point of view.

Unlike us boys,
We have a lot of courage
And strength,
Well some do anyway.
The point is, we are not moany or stupid
We all have knowledge
And we think very
Strongly.

Thank you girls from impatience
Listening to this poem,
Case dismissed!

Imranul Islam (11)
Bacon's College

WAVES

Huge waves crashing into the water,
People in boats looking scared and afraid,
Giant waves look like claws, they're coming to get you
The huge enormous waves as high as the sky.

Bubbles rising to the surface,
The bubbles are balloons popping in the salty, sea air,
The mountain in the distance covered in snow,
Like a giant ice pole.

Samantha Shipman (11)
Bacon's College

THE ROCKY WAVES

Boats surfed on the sea,
Some of them thinking will it be me,
The sea is too rough,
But I'm going to be tough.

Our master cheered us on,
Row faster, but we think he is a con.
The waves grew bigger, but we grew stronger.

We tried to get to land,
But we couldn't even see sand,
We lost 100's of friends,
But we still remember them,
The water splashed in the boats
And we never had no floats.

The sea calmed,
But no one was seen,
Only up there
Angels gleamed.

Emma Kelway (11)
Bacon's College

POEM OF THE CRASHING WAVES

The foam in the waves was just like hands clawing
As the water splashed.
It makes me feel like we are going to smash into the rocks of horror.
The foam felt like snowflakes falling on our skin as we sailed.
It felt like ice tingling down my face
We rowed just as if it was a race.
The foaming hands trying to drag our boat under the sea.
Will we ever survive?

Lucie Thorn (12)
Bacon's College

LOVE

Love is like a sunflower
Blooming in the sun
Love is butterflies
Dancing in your tum.

Love is like a furnace
Burning in your heart
Love is uncontrollable,
Like a work of art.

Love is loyal like a soldier
Waiting to defend
Love will be with you
To the very end.

Love is flowing endlessly
Simple as a rhyme
Love will be in everyone
Till the end of time.

Sam Guile (14)
Bacon's College

THE MYSTERIOUS OCEAN

The wave is like an eagle in the sea
Freezing ice smacking me.
Bubbles increase like foam,
Sometimes I wish I was at home.
The raging sea dragging me,
Is it me?

Matthew Oryang (11)
Bacon's College

MY SEA POEM

The splashing, the crushing,
The wave of power gripped
The minute toy,
As it squeezed the little men.

The splashing, the crushing,
Hovered above the toys.

Lightning and thunder
Rumbled and roared
As the little men became as
Small as a crushed box.

The almighty hand crushed
The last bit of
Sale out of the toys.

Vanessa Agyemang (11)
Bacon's College

THE RAGING SEA

I love the raging sea when it roars,
The waves crash like falling snow.
The sea is as clear as ice.
It is as calm as a raging horse.
It looks like hands, scary ones.
I'm not scare, I love the raging sea.
The sea, so soft.

Carly Hazell (11)
Bacon's College

SCARY

If I could say one thing out loud,
a thing that haunts me at night.
Something I hate so much,
If I could kill it I would.

Darkness
The evil shadows dance across my bedroom wall
and all across my bed.
They dance and chant the moon
and curse the sun.
I love the day it's when all the evil shadows disappear.

But when the night comes,
I just want the ground to swallow me up.

Kay Rozier (11)
Bacon's College

FEAR POEM

Whenever I think of it
My heart begins to pound
My legs go all weak and my
Head spins round and round

I cannot control my feelings
Whenever it is near
I keep telling myself over and over
That there's nothing to fear.

I breakout in a cold sweat
My skin goes all bumpy
Whenever I see a spider
My whole body goes jumpy.

Laura Jane Lennard (12)
Bacon's College

SPELL TO MAKE THE FOOD GO STALE

I put a spell on you,
The fingernail's
Pointed to the food,
It splurted bubbles.
What could we do?
Carrots turned green,
Gravy turned black,
A girl waiting in the queue
Wanted the food so much
She *screamed.*
It was unbearable,
What could I do?
Oops! I've put a spell on you.

Jenny Hodges (11)
Bacon's College

GLITTERING PRIZES

Eye of a newt
Wing of a bat
Football boot,
Tail of a cat!
A branch of a tree,
Some dog's wee,
A mashed up pea
And bread shaped like 'e'!
Mix it 'til it's cold,
Mix it 'til it's old,
Mix it 'til it's nice and bold,
In your hand is precious gold!

Hok Shun (11)
Bacon's College

STRANGE NIGHT

The night was cold and windy
It felt so strange
I started to hear noises
Thinking the window was open
but no, it was shut.
Putting on my sidelight
I still
felt a fright,
trying to sleep
without counting the sheep,
but still I couldn't.
My mind was playing
tricks on me
come on Monique
let's try and sleep.
I put on the radio
to hear some nice tunes
to let my mind
wander away from this doom.
Suddenly I hear
whispering on the stairs
fearing the worst
Monique are you scared?
I opened my bedroom door
there was
by brother
being a big head.

Monique Ayton (11)
Bacon's College

REVENGE

Tomorrow is another day
To make my problems go away.
I'll put a spell on you because of spite
To make all my problems right.
The boys will fall for me
Because you'll be so ugly.
This spell can be broken
Only this will happen
If the man kisses you,
Not just for what you look like,
But your personality.
You will be truly beautiful.

Franki Longman (11)
Bacon's College

PRINCE OF ATLANTA

The edge of the wave was
shaped as a witch's claw.

The foam of the wave was
like biscuits getting crushed into crumbs.

The water poured down as if
there was an avalanche on the mountain.

But I, Prince of Atlanta can
shape the sea, as fountains.

Jeffrey Tieku (11)
Bacon's College

THE WAVE

The wave was a person diving into the deep blue sea.
The foam was a claw, reaching towards me, trying to grab me.
The spray was like ice-cold snow blowing into my face
from the cold night air.
The boat was being tossed from wave to wave,
as I lay in my bed dreaming.
The wave soothed me as I tried to get to sleep.
The wave was a person diving into the deep blue sea.

Melissa Stevens (11)
Bacon's College

WILL I LIVE OR WILL I DIE?

Will I live or will I die? Will I be here tomorrow?
Will I drown or won't I drown?
Maybe I'll make it by tomorrow?
Will I stay in one piece, or will I die in one piece?
Will I see my friends and family or won't I?
The fight goes on but I'll see if I'm here tomorrow.

Gary Hole (12)
Bacon's College

THE WAVE

The waves were as high as mountains.
The sea was like fountains.
The boat shook in the water, while the water swirled around.
The boat was like the leaves when they snap in the autumn.
Bouncing up and down, the Chinese men on the boat
Looked like caterpillars munching on the leaves.

Tom Finch (11)
Bacon's College

NEW BABY BROTHER

I enjoy carrying my baby brother
As I look into his chocolate-brown eyes
They twinkle as if they were diamonds
I feel cheerful when I touch his cute, little hands
As he touches mine.

His special smelling scent of baby lotion
Makes me just want to eat him!
I hear him gurgle, laugh and cry, especially for food
He starts to suck his lips as if that was his bottle,
As if he was eating -
Then he starts to doze, doze, asleep.

Damilola Lasisi Agiri (11)
Bacon's College

THE DEEP BLUE SEA

Crashing, dashing
Decking, wrecking.
The deep, blue sea is angry.
Raging, caving in on boats also floating by.
Claws rippling, water dripping.
The sea is tearing, the deep is wearing
Wood from all the boats.
Roaring, ignoring the men who are sawing
And rowing to try and get going.
I really do wonder where they're going?
And now they're going the sea is glowing
For it will soon be night.

Ian Richardson (11)
Bacon's College

DEBT TO PAY

Will you come with me today?
To you know whom for him to pay
We will meet in a gloomy cave
And then the money we shall save.

Shall we cast a spell on he?
Who has been bad to you and me
You can choose the choice of words
Or instead, use a bunch of swords.

Is it time for us to go
To get the money that he owes?
Should we hit him in the head,
Or stab him twice while in his bed?

Here we are in this old house
Is this the house of the sickly louse?
I will kill him in his room
In the great, huge light of doom.
You will go and get the money
So we can flee to the land of milk and honey.

He is dead; let us leave
He didn't leave till Christmas Eve.

What a shame he had to die
I didn't like his dying cry.

If only his debt did he pay
He would live to see another day.

Hannah Abiola (11)
Bacon's College

Crashing Waves

The waves were crashing together like bricks being launched on top of each other.

The waves looked like a fierce fire-breathing dragon, attacking all of the boats.

All the tough rowers were trying to survive the vicious ocean waves.

The boats were flying up and down in the angry physical waves.

All the little sprays forming as one to make it look like a giant bubble.

James Williams (12)
Bacon's College

Spell For Mind Control

Hairy
Fluffy rabbit
Droppings of a dog bat
Hair and sweat too, I put a spell
On you.

Christy Naish (11)
Bacon's College

FREDDIE KRUEGER

Why do I
Have to be a bad guy?
I'd much rather be with Freddie Junior,
Instead of watching the kids die.
Why can't I have my nails cut once in a while?
They're as sharp as knives,
They're almost a mile.
Why do I have sharp teeth?
They ruin my sexy image,
But they're good at cutting beef!

Blake Richardson (11)
Bacon's College

ENERGY

Every night
People fight.

Every day
People play.

People glare,
People stare.

Why do people have to fight?
Why do people have to play?

Because energy always hits us.

Jermane James Ranson (12)
Bredinghurst School

THE OLD MAN'S LIFE

There was a man
Who lived in a house.
The man was very old
He always had a cold.
The old man's head
Was as big as a ball.
Whatever he did
He drove people up the wall.
He goes on the bus
He does not pay his fares.
He gets thrown off the bus
And nobody cares
If only people would understand
That he was very good with his hands.
That one day he saved my life
When I was just about to be knifed.
Now I stick up for him
When people are rude and stare
At least he knows that somebody cares.

Tyrone Vidal (13)
Bredinghurst School

POETRY LIES SO MUCH

Don't tell me about the meaning of life,
Don't tell me anything at all.
Don't tell me what to do,
Don't you tell me any of your lies.
Again and again you tell me lies,
I am tired.

Poetry lies so much.

Anton Jacques (13)
Bredinghurst School

The Body In The Park

A body was laying on the damp ground
Half uncovered waiting to be found.
Her clothes all bloody and torn
Her shoes well weathered and worn.

Her purse empty and open wide
How she must have screamed and cried.
Lipstick smeared across her face
Laying beside her a hanky made of lace.

As she laid there next to her brolly
I bet the killer won't be sorry.

Her eye's cold and lifeless, nothing to be seen
They were the most amazing, amazing colour green.

Lee Jarvis (15)
Bredinghurst School

A Shoe

I am a shoe, but not to be worn.
I have no stretch marks from nasty corns.

I'm part of a collection of arty design ranging from
Gucci to Clarks but they're all friends of mine.

If a person wants to try me they have to freshen up
Because I have a smell of finery,
I don't want to mess up.

People like me for my classy look and some people
Put me in something called a catalogue book.

I can make people taller with my fashionable heel
That bends onwards and outwards for maturity appeal.

Lauren Green (15)
Catford Girls School

LOVE

Love is precious
Love is sweet
Love is like something to eat
Love is hatred
Love is tender
Love is like a big wonder.

Love is precious
Love is sweet
Why people like love really gets me
Love is hatred
Love is tender
Love is like a real bother.

Love is precious
Love is sweet
Love is like why it ain't with me
Love is hatred
Love is tender
Love is really wild with pleasure.

Love is precious
Love is sweet
Have you got love?
Love is hatred
Love is tender
I have love
Do you love me?

Sharnell Marcelle (16)
Catford Girls School

I Think I'm Too Nice

I think I'm too nice,
Is that what you say,
When I hold my head high
Turn a blind eye
To the people that say
She's a B****.

I think I'm too nice,
Is that what you say?
Cause you know that
I'll be somewhere
A year from today.

I think I'm too nice,
Cause I have an ambition
A goal to reach
And haven't got time
For silly games.

I think I'm too nice, yeah?
Oh
I think I'm too nice.

Charlene Keyes (15)
Catford Girls School

Going Round The Roundabout

What goes round the roundabout?
A car, a bike and a bus.
What goes round the roundabout?
A truck, a lorry and a bicycle.
What goes round the roundabout?

Scott Mizzi (11)
Chestnut Grove School

LITTLE MOUSE

You are so small
Little mouse, little mouse.

You are so quiet,
Little mouse, little mouse.

So cute, so fair,
With grey hair,
You are so little,
Little mouse, little mouse.

You have brown eyes,
Little mouse, little mouse.

The wall is your house,
Little mouse, little mouse.

You are covered in fleas and
You nibble on cheese,
That is your life,
Little mouse, little mouse.

Ben Simpson (12)
Chestnut Grove School

SLAVERY

S   hips took them away,
L   oved ones left astray,
A   wful times are what they had,
V   ile, disgusting and bad.
E   ach person didn't know what they did,
R   ifles were even shot at kids,
Y   ?

Jordan Edge (13)
Chestnut Grove School

TEN AGES OF MAN

Crying, crawling and rolling around,
Calling for Mum, barking like a hound.
Skipping, jumping little girl,
Ballet lessons, learning how to twirl.
Homework, homework, all day long,
Just work, work, work you don't even get paid.
Secondary School's maybe Chestnut Grove.
I'm so desperate I'm jumping on the pavement,
Going to a party eating Smarties
Can't stop till you drop.
Maybe I'll have a baby, I'll name the lovie Debbie,
I'm getting really old and my lovie is cold.
The house is all stinky and the walls have mould.
Now is the time to cover my shine
Because now I have to lie as I wait to die,
As I start to cry as I say goodbye to my lovie.

Helena Vidot (12)
Chestnut Grove School

WEDDING DAY

The bells are ringing in the church,
The sun is shining through the trees,
The bride is walking really slowly,
It's one big happy day for her,
She's getting married to her prince,
The sun is shining in their lives.

It's going to be happy days for us
And after that the party starts all night,
But after 20 years they still as one
And always will be.

Galina Gorlova (11)
Chestnut Grove School

THE OLYMPICS
(Dedicated to my dad)

Adrenaline Rush

I trained and trained whilst it rained and rained
But it was worth all the power I gained and gained,
Three months later I got a letter with a brand new GB
Sweater, what an adrenaline rush, I couldn't get enough.
I wanted more and more and more so I jumped
Up and down on my bedroom floor.
I began screaming out for more.
That's when I got the feeling I'm gonna win gold,
I was looking big, proud and bold,
So I was off to Sidney Harbour to win
That gold for me and my father so all the people
At Sidney Harbour will remember the day,
I won gold for me and my father.

Callum Campbell (12)
Chestnut Grove School

WHAT KIND OF

What kind of work would you like to do,
When you are all grown up and not in school,
Would you like to be a doctor who helps make people well?
Would you like to be a salesman with something fine to sell?

Would you like to be a pilot flying high up in the air
Or a fireman?
Or a policeman helping people everywhere?
Would you like to teach nice boys and girls
To read and write and spell?
But whatever job you choose to do, work hard and do it well.

Louis Wright (15)
Chestnut Grove School

I Wanna Be A Star

I wanna be a star,
I wanna go far,
I wanna drive around,
In a big black car.
I said yeah I wanna be a star.

I wanna be a hit,
I wanna be it,
I wanna see my name,
All brightly lit
I said yeah I wanna be a hit.

I wanna be on the screen,
I wanna be the scene,
I wanna see my face,
On the cover of a magazine.
I said yeah I wanna be on the screen.

I wanna be a star,
I wanna go far,
But I've only got a
Job in a burger bar
So far!

Reece Rose (12)
Chestnut Grove School

Night And Day

Night and day
Have a funny way
Of making an impression
At one you sleep
You snuggle deep
To wash away depression.

When you wake up
You sup, sup, sup,
At your fresh orange juice,
You get up and go
Get with the flow,
But make sure your trousers aren't loose.

Alexander Martin (12)
Chestnut Grove School

MY POEM

Eat an orange,
Sing a song,
Don't touch a bee
As it buzzes along.
Run for an hour and
You can walk for a day,
Talk to the birds and animals
And don't forget to listen
To what they say.
So watch the wind and
Always listen to the moon.
Hear the rain play
Its magical tune,
A camp site of fire,
Keeps the wolves away
And a brand new pair of blue
Shoes is worth an hour of play.
So go over the cloudy mountains
Which runs the way to Chestnut School,
He or she who will not take this way
Lives and dies a stupid fool.

Gemma Moram (12)
Chestnut Grove School

THE GARDEN

The garden is a wonderful place
In my honour and grace.
There are flowers, grass, some pots of brass
But there are hardly any trees. There is one lonely
Tree that has hardly any leaves but when children
Come the tree now blooms and there are hardly any
Gloom, the tree brings life for you, no one should bring
A knife to this tree but if it dies, I will lie about
The flowers grass, brass and gloom and I will say there was
No tree or I will make people pay a fee to see a tree
With bloom and no gloom.
The garden is a wonderful place in my honour and my grace.

Hollie Graham (12)
Chestnut Grove School

MY COUSIN

My cousin is bald,
Because he's only 3 weeks old,
His eyes are small
And his nose is like a button,
His mouth, his mouth is a black hole.

His hands are a soft white towel,
His feet are the colour of a pink rose,
His ears are cold and pink.

But my favourite part of my cousin
Is his body because it is a soft fluffy
White pillow.

Gemma Tester (12)
Chestnut Grove School

I Asked . . .

I asked the little girl who cannot see
'What is colour like?' She replied.

Red is the colour of angry and frustration,
Blue is the colour of the coldness within some people.

Yellow is the colour of brightness and summer.

Pink is the colour of a sweet smelling rose.

Purple is the colour of my soul.

Love is the colour of my heart,
Black is the colour I see . . .

Chantelle Mason (15)
Chestnut Grove School

I Know

I know how it feels to get looked in the eyes,
I know just why clouds go dark in the sky.
I know why lakes just wave and flow,
I know just why birds fly so low.

I know that doves always fly in two,
I know that dreams just don't come true,
I know how and why we die,
I know that my head is always high.

But what I would like to know is,
How this world became so bold?
I know we all come and go,
I just wish the world would go so slow.

Kelly Plaine (12)
Chestnut Grove School

THE NEW MILLENNIUM 2000

The new millennium let us see
What it has in store for you and me.

Family and friends won't be split apart,
The millennium shall bring us a brand new start.

People should start to put things right, start acting proper,
Stop getting into fights.

We should make up a brand new law
That death and pain shall be no more.

People won't be judged by what they wear
They should be treated equal and fair.

All wars shall have to cease
People of all nations will unite in peace.

When troubles and pain go away
Peace and love shall be here to stay.

At the end of the day that is what I think
That the new millennium shall to us bring.

Michael Delahaye (12)
Chestnut Grove School

NATIONAL POETRY DAY

Weather

It was really, really hot one day,
So all my friends came out to play.

My mummy told me to come inside,
I said 'No I'm staying outside!'

Shantelle Patricia Collins (12)
Chestnut Grove School

FEAR!

Fear is . . . being scared but not always bad or
For good, fear makes you stop and think.
Fear is . . . your heart pounding and bounding in your chest
Faster and faster, fear pricking at your skin right
Down to your bone.
Fear is . . . something that can change your mind,
Fear punishes you.
Stop, think, proceed, fear is . . .
Uncertain like being alone in the dark,
Fear is not unforeseen,
Fear can change your life, fear can take over your body.

Fear!

Fear is . . . something that everyone has
Your heart pounds and bounds inside your chest.
Fear is . . . something that can change your life.
Fear is . . . something that pricks your skin down to your bone,
Fear is . . . being scared but not always for bad or for good,
Fear makes you stop and think,
Fear can change your life forever.

Hülya Hassan & Camilla Evans (11)
Chestnut Grove School

MY POEM

I painted a picture for you to see,
I plucked a rose for you to smell,
I planted grass for you to touch.

But you didn't see my picture
And you didn't smell my rose.
But you didn't touch my grass.

Courtney Ferlance (12)
Chestnut Grove School

FRIENDSHIP

Ingredients:

1 pail of love,
2 barrels of laughter,
6 tablespoons of caring,
1 litre of thoughtfulness and
8 teaspoons of trust and smiles.

First take 3 tablespoons of caring and a barrel of
Laughter, whip lightly, add the 1 litre of thoughtfulness and
Heat till piping hot, add the other 3 tablespoons of caring
Your mixture should be forming.
Add 8 teaspoons of trust and smile and stir,
Add your pail of love, add the barrel of laughter
And your mixture should be ready, the friendship should last forever.

Natasha Patterson-Waugh (12)
Chestnut Grove School

THE WORLD'S MIGRAINE

'Twas on a dark and stormy night,
When all were hoping it would be bright.
The angry thunder was raging on,
The world's migraine,
Can't bear the light of the sun.

Never bright, never bright,
People praying inside their homes,
Shouting to the God they think is there,
Please be light, please be light.

Bashing, flashing, rolling, destroying,
Everything in the world to be seen,
Uprooting trees, wrecking buildings,
The world will never again be green.

Nick East (12)
Chestnut Grove School

PSYCHOTIC SISTER

My sister that poor old thing,
Tells me all of her wild fantasies,
She even saves her dirtiest socks for her best occasions
And tells me when she changes them.
Yuk!
She even tells me when I should brush my teeth
And that's once every year,
Gosh what sort of sister is that?
Does she care?

My sister, that maniac, has flies for pets,
Rats for friends and pigeons for neighbours,
She even feeds them every day.

My sister that football hooligan,
Even thinks that one day David Beckham would
Ask her to play on the Manchester United team.
Please!

My sister, who picks her nose because her ears are tickling,
Says she can see everything that goes on behind her.

She's a real alien! Isn't she?

Ruth N'Choh (11)
Chestnut Grove School

FED UP

I'm fed up.

I'm fed up with seeing people choking
With black exhaust fumes from cars,
Choking and coughing their lungs out to death.

I'm angry.

I'm angry that humans kill their own species
And that people do things on purpose
And lie about it so much.

I'm annoyed.

I'm annoyed that wars are started over things
That can be talked about quite easily.

I'm slightly upset.

I'm slightly upset about the poverty, disease
And death that surrounds us in the world
And that, one day, someone will put a stop to it.

I'm happy.

I'm happy that some people do notice these things
And sometimes put it right.

When oh when will the world realise?

The question remains.

James Armian (11)
Chestnut Grove School

KING OF THE RING

The music plays, he emerges, every night,
He could die,
He would rather do this than die.
The competition emerges
Both drive by their urges,
The bell rings
Who will be king.
Both start to fight
It will be very tight,
They go to the top of the turnbuckle
Will they plummet?
A foot tips,
Both bodies totally tip
Both are down,
They really want that crown
One arm moves,
1 . . . 2 . . . a shoulder goes up,
The match continues
He picks him up
But quick as a hiccup
He falls over,
1 . . . 2 . . . if only the ref. counted quicker,
Again, this fight
Is very tight,
Then suddenly, he hits his finish
1 . . . 2 . . . 3 . . . it's all over.
Both shake and embrace in the ring
There can only be one but just then
They both were king.

Paul Clayton (11)
Chestnut Grove School

THE APPLE

The apple and core,
The centre of my universe,
The beginning, middle and end.

The stalk is my umbilical cord,
Severed and I was expelled
Into this cruel uncertain world.

The skin,
The outer crust,
The foundation I am surrounded in,
With the security, love and affection
From my family.

The texture is the rough times that awaits
Me or appears when I least expect it.

Sweet flesh. The happy times in my life,
New loves, weddings, births and achievements.

And the core, the end,
The death,
The afterlife.

Roena Williams (14)
Chestnut Grove School

SEASIDE

As I look out of my window I see a coastline that
Used to be so beautiful in the summer, but now winter's
Here, it's all changed.

The waves overlap each other like the sea Olympics and then
Clash together with the rocks to perform an amazing water feature.

The sand stays still, holding on to the other grains before the
Wicked wind of the west blows their friends to the other
End of the beach.

The wind whistles a deceiving tune to all those that fall for it.

The mist is a blanket that covers the coastline like a
Barrier and stops its beauty from being seen.

The clouds churn to the beat of the wind and
Illuminates the sky with dull colours.

Fortresses were blown into sandcastles which were bombed
By the heartless west winds on the sea front.

The local chippy closes down for the winter and goes in
Search of a more warm climate, Greece is on the agenda.

Raymond Yuill (14)
Chestnut Grove School

Love

Love is when two people care,
Love is when two people stare,
Love is when two people go to bed,
Love is when two people wake up,
Love is when two people argue,
Love is when two people cuddle,
Love is when two people share,
Love, love, love
Is love.

Gemma Currell (11)
Chestnut Grove School

Love Or Loneliness

Sitting, waiting, by the door,
Playing with me dinky cars on the floor.

In comes someone through the door,
Not even noticing me on the floor.
Stepping over me, like I'm a bore.

Waiting for me mum to come in,
All I see is Dad and Mona.

What about me?

Victor Ohene (13)
Crofton School

It's His Own Fault

First he made me . . .
Stitching and sewing evil to evil.
Second, he ran off and left me.
He wanted to kill me so why did he create me?
I wandered the streets being beaten and battered.
Dogs barked, bit and attacked,
I travelled to the forest where I found happiness.
But it ended bitterly.
I was abandoned again.
Revenge.
I must have revenge.
I killed his brother and framed his loyal friend for it.
On his wedding night I killed his wife because he denied me mine,
I punched my fist through her chest and ripped out her heart.

It's his own fault . . .

Samice Morris (12)
Crofton School

School Rules

I graf on the door
And I paint on the floor,
Oh no, I've broken the school law!
I am a star and I am a sizer.
Michael is a smooth dog
And he is a groove dog.
Ben is the presser
He's a heavy dresser.

Airam Myrie (11)
Crofton School

MY FAMILY

My mum
Is not dumb,
My dad
Is not mad.
My sister
Is not as clever as Dexter,
My brother
There is no other.
I have a dog
And a mog
I have a dish
With five fish.
I have two birds
Not nerds.
I have two pigs
Guinea pigs.
I have a hamster
Who is a gangster
And then there's me
Plain old me.

Donna McVitie (12)
Crofton School

IF

If I had a magic bicycle,
I'd fly up to the moon,
My teacher thinks I'm reading,
But I'm really feeding a baboon.

You may think it's a poem,
But that's not the truth,
This poem was written by
An alien under my flat roof.

Now you may think this
Poem must have been
Easy to write but
Gorillas and kangaroos
Where jumping through the night.

Now I must say these
Last words before the aliens come
Beware of your teachers
You don't know if they're human.

Natasha Baptiste (11)
Crofton School

OCEAN

The ocean is unpredictable.
What lies at the bottom is enchanted
And holds a lot of wonders.
It can be calm and peaceful
And at other times it can be rough and treacherous!
The waves clash viciously against the rocks
Like thunder and lightning.
The ocean is crystal-clear,
Like a shining bright star.
Waves tumble over each other
Like a trees branches brushing against a garden fence.
The deep blue sea is cold and salty.
Seaweed floats across
Like a leaf being thrown across the ground.
The sea is like the Earth:
There are loads of fish in the sea
And there are loads of people on Earth.
The colour blue is a cold and icy colour
Like the beautiful sight of the Antarctic.

Ricky Ryan (12)
Crofton School

A Dream That's Real!

Context: School bullies - victim of bullying.

I stand here upon the playground floor
And I hear a powerful almighty roar,
It's the sound of a terrible fighting mob
They're coming closer, oh my God.
Their voices poisoning my brain and mind
Why me I am so nice and kind?
Their taunting voices give me a headache,
I stand here waiting for my fate.
Their shadows now fall upon my head,
Huh! Oh - I'm in my bed,
It turns out to be just a dream.
But I know the real world is just as mean.

Jamiel Thomas (13)
Crofton School

Kissing

As I write a letter to Mum
I hear a rumble in my tum,
I go downstairs to get some food,
I suddenly realise I was not in the mood,
As I wait and anticipate,
I decide to go anyway.

I look in the mirror,
What do I see?
My father and Mona kissing
In front of me.

Lisa Holmes (13)
Crofton School

She Wishes

My teacher thinks I'm reading
But really I am daydreaming,
About being a dragon fighter,
Or maybe something even mightier.
How about a DJ
Or I might be going somewhere far, far away,
Maybe I can be a juggler,
Juggling around my balls,
Maybe a singer,
One that makes others look like fools.
Got to go Pips have gone.
Oh no!

Dariye Havutcu
Crofton School

A Poem About Ghosts

Ghosts are weary,
Ghosts are scary,
Ghosts like shouting 'Boo!'
Ghosts like to watch you jump and scream!
Although they're not that scary on the screen.
You may not know that a ghost will never say hello,
A ghost will float by you'll scream and maybe start to cry.
But you will never stop and shy and ghosts should never make you cry,
A ghost is someone who had died but doesn't know how to say their
Goodbyes.

Eloise Dickie
Crofton School

POEM

What have I done?
I must be mad
Have I done something good or something bad?
I did not want this
I did not ask for this
I would have wanted my monster
To live in bliss anything but this
It would have wanted a hug it would have wanted kiss
But all these wondrous things he shall miss
Poor creature, poor creature
With more than one ugly feature.

Luther Alcide-Coghiel (12)
Crofton School

MY DREAM

My teacher thinks I'm reading
But I'm really in Timbuktu
I'm having a sword-fight
And I don't really know what to do.
The three-headed monsters are coming
Two by two!
I'm stabbing them in the chest ...
Well, what would you do?

Emma Tapley (11)
Crofton School

Who Am I?

Who am I? I don't know,
What am I? A monster guess so,
Why am I here? To try not to hate!

What I don't know
Why did Frankenstein make me if he
Was only going to abandon me.

I have no food,
I have to eat people's trash.

It does not matter,
OK that means that I'm alive.

Dean Constantinou (12)
Crofton School

The Monster

Where am I?
What am I?
Who am I?
What am I doing here?
Why am I here?
Something is nipping me!
Why am I in pain,
I am alive!

Hulya (12)
Crofton School

Autumn

Crisp leaves crunching underfoot,
Early sun burning through damp mists,
Frozen dewdrops glisten, scattered jewels in the sun,
Fat blackberries shaken by soft breezes.
Robin swoops to brown fields trying to claw a meal,
Rain clouds overhead, drizzle forms a rainbow.

Soft rain stops as evening comes, sun sets,
Orange, yellow and red veil the sky,
Naked boughs, trees dance in moonlight,
Darkness creeps upon autumn's unsuspecting days.

Zara Frith (12)
Emanuel School

The Bullfight

A bull stands lonely in the field at night,
Not knowing that soon it will be taken to fight.
It chews at the grass, its colours brown and white,
Not knowing that soon it will be taken to fight.
It's freezing and shivers with coldness not fright,
Not knowing that soon it will be taken to fight.
Darkness surrounds it, not an inch of light,
Not knowing that soon it will be taken to fight.
A bull stands in the arena with not a single right,
It knows it's going to die in a bullfight.

Justin Moll (12)
Emanuel School

Got You!

It was snowing.
The icy polar winds blew bitter and cold
A man below looked up at the bleak grey sky.
Bare trunks with only brown to show.
He walked away
The snow subsided, the lamps came on
The man reappeared with a boy alongside.
He bent down and rose again, brandishing a snowball.
He hurled it at the little boy
An eerie shriek could be heard.
The boy turned to a wall,
In one quick movement he pelted the snowball
Right in his father's face.

'Got you!'

Marcus Aitman (12)
Emanuel School

Summer

As I sunbathe on the soft, glittery sand,
While I sip a refreshing drink,
The smells I smell are of freshly cut grass,
With the salty smell of the sea,
The sea lies ahead of me . . .
The grass lies behind me . . .
The birds and I lie inbetween . . .
With my imagination running wild.
The sun is sizzling and burning,
Like someone getting sunburnt,
The sunset's late . . .
Scorching and flaming in the bright pink sky.

Samantha Lewis-Purkis (12)
Emanuel School

HIROSHIMA - THE BIRTH OF A MONSTER

It was in August 45
That the atomic bomb exploded
Both nature and men died
But this monster stayed alive.

Invented by the Americans,
Helped by Einstein,
This poor genius
Ignored what he'd done.

It was a victory for the west
And for the Allied Nations
The east were defeated
And so was mankind.

The atomic bomb didn't end:
It killed till '89
Because of greedy powers
Who threatened to kill and conquer the world.

Guillaume Lincoln (13)
Lycée Français Charles De Gaulle School

SEASHORE

The arms of the sea
Disappear on the shore
Where the seaweed lies
And of thirst, slowly dies.

Jessica White (13)
Lycée Français Charles De Gaulle School

A Grim Visit

It was on a foggy day
That Kirt took his last breath,
He innocently walked in the street
But around the corner, was death.

Memories of those he killed came back
But even now the war was never over
As screaming faces appeared in his mind
He couldn't help but shiver.

But still he made another mistake,
As he walked into the police station
He took an air gun with him
And pointed it without caution.

He threatened the police, he threatened the law
And now the tears blinded his eyes
For he knew what would happen
Because he had not been wise.

They asked him to put his gun down
But he did not listen
Now, the time had come
And his courage had risen.

As the bullet tore through the air
He never had time to say, 'Bye,'
To those he cared about
Before he had to die.

Stephanie Foin (13)
Lycée Français Charles De Gaulle School

THE MURDER OF SARAH PAYNE

Sarah was at the countryside
Staying for the weekend
At her grandmother's house,
With her family but no friends.

She wanted to play with her sisters
But they said 'No' and told her off
And so an argument started
And then she ran off.

They told her to come back
But Sarah kept on running
So they went inside
And said nothing.

They called the police
While her mother was crying,
After half an hour of looking
They'd found nothing.

The police found her body
Naked, dirty and dead,
'Who has done this to her?'
Her mother said.

They tried to find the murderer
To lock him up in jail
But it was going to be hard
Because he never left a trail.

Natalia Boolaky (13)
Lycée Français Charles De Gaulle School

THE BALLAD OF MANDY VICTIM OF THE SEA

Mandy swims daily
In the deep blue sea
But today's the last
'Cause away she will pass.

As she sets foot in the water
She doesn't see her killer
Waiting in the deep
Looking fast asleep.

Mandy is swimming
Swimming gracefully
Not realising
She's at its mercy.

The water is dark
The water is deep
She can't see the shark
Ready for the sweep.

Emerging from the foam
Its jaw wide open
Chews away the bones
Eats the poor woman.

Mandy screams
Mandy cries
The shark kills
And she dies.

Alison Novic (13)
Lycée Français Charles De Gaulle School

The Secret Of The Shark

The sun was shining bright
And the surfers were alright
On Aussie's Bondi Beach
Where sharks seldom reach.

But our hero, Barry Pott
Was feeling rather hot
So he took his surfing board
To make a new record.

The shark was slick and silent,
A veritable giant
King of all the oceans
With unknown emotions.

Barry swam and swam,
His board stuck like a clam,
Searching for a big wave,
He thought he was so brave.

'Sharky' slowly followed,
Snapped and slowly swallowed.
They did not hear a sound
Only a surfboard found.

The 23rd of September
Everyone will remember
On Aussie's Bondi Beach
Where sharks seldom reach.

Alexandra Michell (13)
Lycée Français Charles De Gaulle School

BALLAD OF JODIE AND MARY

Jodie and Mary arrived on time
Their parents were so pleased,
Until the doctor told them
Their daughters are 'Siamese.'

Their parents struggled with the shock
Then felt they had to know,
What were the implications?
How would their children grow?

The doctor then gave them
The worst news he could impart,
That one twin was quite healthy
And the other had no heart.

So now they have a choice,
No parent should have to make
To allow one twin to die
For the other one's sake.

The doctors took this to court
To let them make a decision.
The judges decided to separate
Would be the best solution.

So this is the end
Of a very tragic story,
But life will shine and shimmer
In Mary's sister Jodie.

Corinne Smart (12)
Lycée Français Charles De Gaulle School

VOLCANO

It was on Sunday morning that Matthew woke up
He was trembling and shaking which made him sit up
It was still very early and there was no sun
But he got up anyway to have some fun.

Quickly he dressed ready for a cold day
As it had been snowing since the day before yesterday
He thought he might go and see his friend Arnaud
Maybe have a snowball fight while the conditions were right.

He went out the front door and walked into the street
But then he saw something that made his heart beat
Because from up on the hill came a river of red
While all the people of the town were still lying in bed.

Matthew ran back to the house to go tell his daddy
He returned to his house because he wanted his mummy
I ran back to the room and went to Daddy's bed
I told him about the volcano but he said 'Go back to bed.'

I told him it was for real so he looked out the window
He turned back to Mummy but what he said was hard to follow
Daddy called the police and we all got in the car
And hurried down the road and tried to get far.

Later we were all safe far away from the fire
But where had Arnaud gone I tried to enquire
Had he gone somewhere else to escape from the flames
Or stayed at that place where they were calling his name.

'Arnaud has gone' the policeman said
He went to a better place to where the fire had led'
Arnaud hadn't known a thing up there in his bed
And he felt no pain as he became red.

James Haydon (13)
Lycée Français Charles De Gaulle School

THE CONCORDE CRASH

As the hour of departure came
The passengers stood in line
The flight attendants asked for their names
As they boarded the death plane.

The pilot was in his cockpit
Waiting for the permission
While all the passengers
Got into their position.

When Concorde got up in the air
There was a sign of tranquillity
The flight attendants were about to take care
Of the passengers behind.

It wasn't long before the pilot heard of the disaster
He called and was told his wheel was on fire.

The pilot knew what was coming
There was nowhere to land the plane
Most of the passengers were napping
Not knowing and not prepared for dying.

The Concorde crashed on a hotel nearby
And all around you could see people cry
All the other companies with Concorde's closed that day
To be sure that won't happen again.

Alexander Maudhuit (13)
Lycée Français Charles De Gaulle School

THE TRAGEDY THAT SHOCKED US ALL

'Twas on a Sunday afternoon
While playing with her friends
That Sarah disappeared from home
To never be seen again.

Sarah had been playing
When up had come a man,
He talked to and befriended her
She was bundled into his van.

Sarah she was six years old
And wearing a blue dress
Her parents said she was all smiles
They called her their 'princess'.

Sarah went missing for over a month,
Before she was dramatically found:
Her body bruised, her clothes half-ripped
Lying dead on the ground.

The country went into mourning
The tragedy caused national outcry
I'm sure we all think that when he is caught
The murderer deserves to die.

So let us all silently pray
That some day he'll suffer in prison
And the little girl who captured all our hearts,
Is happy up above in Heaven.

Giannina Kline (13)
Lycée Français Charles De Gaulle School

THE TITANIC

On the night of the 12th
A ship set sail,
The biggest in its class
'Twas as big as a whale.

Halfway through the journey
An iceberg hit the front
And all the excited passengers
Had a terrible bump.

As the damage increased,
A hole got bigger and bigger
And as the water unleashed,
It became an enormous river.

The captain said it was nothing;
He lied.
A gigantic wave swept him off,
He died.

And as the boat sunk faster
The decks they started to bend
And all was a disaster;
The dream came to an end.

As the cold wind blows
And the red sun sets,
There'll always be something
Lying beneath the depths.

Raphaël Rashid (13)
Lycée Français Charles De Gaulle School

FATE OF THE CONCORDE

Mothers, fathers and children flee,
With thoughts of holiday fun,
Upon The Concorde in the sun
Unknowing what their fate would be.

As the flagship of avionics took off,
It resembled a flying swan.
Never anything had gone wrong,
But that song was soon to end.

Speeding out from Charles de Gaulle,
Looking like a comet
With a tail of fire out of one jet
It met its forthcoming doom,
That brought sadness to all.

Destiny controlled the bird,
Its destiny bloomed -
The plane was doomed
Panic aboard was heard.

Altitude and stability lost,
It twisted and twirled through the air,
Barely missing the hotel
Where finally finding its death
On the stony ground beneath.

For months and months the experts surmised
To determine the plane's demise,
But alas, it was with a simple tyre-burst
That fate destroyed those hundred lives.

Nathaniel Carter (13)
Lycée Français Charles De Gaulle School

THE TITANIC

The great black hull towering over the quay side
The people scurrying like ants on the deck below
The crowd waving their white hands by the side
The tiny boats bringing the big monster in tow.

The cruiser sped on towards the night,
The fateful night of dread
The white ice mountain glowing in the light.
The single cry 'iceberg ahead!'

The screeching metal, the scraping ice
The slow low tear in the ship
The screaming people and worst . . .
The silence afterwards.

The few survivors hanging on
Until the morning break
With dawn new hopes are always born
White foam slushing in its wake.

The scramble to get on
The tears and wails
As slowly very slowly
The ghastly truth prevails.

Hugo Minchin (13)
Lycée Français Charles De Gaulle School

GOING HOME

Made it out
Paid out my coins.
The neon lights
Are humming.
Fed my slip,
The engine's whirl
And now the train
Is coming.
The cellphones ring,
The lovers lie
The suit sweats tears
With matching tie
That's loosened round his
Collar bone.
But that's OK, I'm going home.
The Walkmans sing
Their techno beats
Beneath the grey polluted streets
But I hear nothing
I am immune
I'm levitating, meditating
That's OK, I'll be home soon.

Claire Thompson (12)
Lycée Français Charles De Gaulle School

OLYMPICS

One day they left, they took the plane
To the country deep down under
Hard they had worked and for many hours
And now all they wanted was to conquer.

A boy called Torpedo set the pace
17 years old, so they say.
How the Aussies cheered as he won the race
And then did the same the very next day.

In another part of Sydney
An American hero, Marion Jones
She ran so fast so therefore
Three golds and bronzes she now owns.

The fireworks set the city alight
The athletes' emotions were running high
Sydney Harbour shone so bright
As they said their fond farewells.

Hannah Creasey (13)
Lycée Français Charles De Gaulle School

I Like

I like my cat
and stroke it
all the time

Cat always
miaow, miaow
and play with
string and little ball

Scratch, scratch
on the chair,
creep under the
table and purr, purr,
paw and paw on his face

Soft fluffy and
playful lying
sprawled on the
carpet and

yawning sleep zzzzzzz

Karen Kelly (15)
Oak Lodge School

Believing In My Own Peace

At night
Funky clothes
Bright light flashing
Red, green, yellow

Through midnight
Rap dancing - thrum
Drum beating
Rain drop, thrum, thrum

Early morning
Winding down
Whirr . . . whooo . . . wuss down . . .

    Believing in my own peace
    Believing in my own peace
    In rap

Clive Young (15)
Oak Lodge School

SKY TIMELESS SONG

Bird's wings soar high
and bird's wings dive low
but sky-sky timeless
sky timeless
sky timeless
sky timeless
sky timeless

Aeroplane's engine come loud
and aeroplane's engine go quiet
but sky-sky timeless
sky timeless
sky timeless
sky timeless
sky timeless

Butterfly birth flitter and floating
and butterfly death leaden sky moaning
but sky-sky timeless
sky timeless
sky timeless
sky timeless
sky timeless

Jani Begum (14)
Oak Lodge School

READY DANCE

Black dance cha-cha-cha
Black dance foxtrot
Black dance rumba
Black dance samba
Black dance tango
Black dance waltz

Choo choo choo!
Rap! Rap! Rap!
Choo choo choo!
Kablam pow!
Wham! Smack! Thwark!
One two three.

Faheem Malik (15)
Oak Lodge School

I LIKE

I like to remember
Swimming, sea shimmering
Like a mirror, clear
But sea breakers, swell.

Driving rain, drum beat
Rap, thrum, thrum, thrum
Inky sky, billowing clouds
Sheet of lightning - shriek.

Sun come to calm, soothing
Peaceful, quiet, restful,
'Time for me football.'

Seon Anderson (15)
Oak Lodge School

BULLYING

A Bully!

A bully is like a snake all slimy and slivering,
He is like thunder a loud strong roar
He is like an uppercut delivered from Mike Tyson strong and firm
He is like a spike sharp and dangerous
He is strong hard and solid
He is like laughter mean and spiteful

A Victim!

A victim is like a sheep lost from its shepherd
He is like the sound of crying a chanting moan
He is like a leaf pushed by the wind
He is like a ball curled up tight
He is weak and vulnerable
He is lonely and a main target.

Rebecca Penfold (14)
Riverston School

ANGER

It is a velociraptor it is a carnivore like a T-rex
It kills carnivores that invade its nest
It moves quickly very fast
Like a cheetah and jumps like a kangaroo
It is a burning red animal
It is striped brown and black
It is a rival it acts like a catapult
It is thundering, it sounds like a gorilla
It is horrible.

This is *anger*

Courtney Riley (11)
Riverstone School

BULLIES

Bully, bully girl, boy, woman or man
They are coming to get you if they can

They call you names, pull faces too
They are really cowards, trying to frighten you

They enjoy your upset and think it's right
To torment you and want to fight

A kick, or punch or a slap they do
They only want to pick on you

You feel afraid and very depressed
But tell someone it is the best

You can feel lonely, unhappy and sad
If they would only stop, you would feel glad

You ignore their name-calling, you really try
But the very next day they make you cry

When will it stop, I want to know
And then my fear will suddenly go

Bullies are here, bullies are there
Bullies are really everywhere.

Lianne Hemblade (13)
Riverston School

ANGER

It is a Tyrannosaurus Rex
With razor sharp teeth.

It moves roughly
Like when it's fighting its meal.

Anger is black
Like when you turn off your light.

It's a saw or a drill
Cutting through metal.

It is fast rap sounds of shouting
Shouting at the top of your voice.

This is anger.

Ashley Thanni (11)
Riverston School

TODAY

Today,
What is today?
A day, an hour, a piece of historic time,
Yesterday didn't seem the day for me
But today, I have decided that I will surely
Reach my prime.

Yesterday,
What was yesterday?
A short day that just passed by,
A day that went by just with that split second.
But then what keeps us from the future
And the past.

Tomorrow,
What is tomorrow?
Will it ever arrive or come?
Do we ever know when it will be?
Or is it a day you decide to flee from
Or a day you decide to look forward to?
What will I do tomorrow?
What will happen tomorrow?
Will tomorrow ever come.

Oluwafemi Okulaja (14)
Riverston School

TRUTH

The truth enables us to stay and cling to the earth
Sort of how static electricity works
See, truth brings light
Light retracts off a mirror.

Visions of yourself as an error could never be clearer,
The truth is that you're ugly, not on the outside
But on the inside, on the outside you boast that you're lovely.
These things are all well hidden,
But when you're in denial of self it's forbidden, that' the truth.

On my neck, I've still got marks from the bullets
The truth produces fear that has people running like Carl Lewis
Names will be on the lips of dying men
If ever crushed in the earth, they shall rise again.
words of lying men, sounding lush like a violin.

To bring the light to the dark, breathe some light in the art.
This must be the truth, because we keep moving on,
The truth lays the foundation of what we rocket on.
You can't see it if you're blind, but we'll always prevail
Life is like an open sea, the truth is the wind in our sail.

Femi Sijuade (15)
Riverston School

SCHOOL BLUES

I hate school I really do
Every day there is nothing new
Just do your work and do your best
The marks must be good in today's test.

I get up late in the morning
And get to school still yawning
Today will be cross-country in the rain
Is there no respite from this pain?

When I get home it's always dark
I say to myself let's go to the park
Yet I check my watch and it's already late
Is boredom to be my fate?

When I leave school and I open my front door
I see a letter on the floor
I open it and the news says you've passed
I got all my GCSE's at last.

Gavin Shirley (15)
Riverston School

MY LOVE FOR HIM

My love for him is greater than life
The first time I met you it was love at first sight
I never knew you felt the same
I hesitated to approach you, but now I wish I did
You met someone else and fell in love
My heart was broken, but I blamed no one but myself
I cried every day when I saw you with her
You're the first person I ever felt like this about
I feel so far away from you, yet you are so close
Or maybe it's because you're all the way in Africa, anyhow,
I know I loved you, and still love you and always will love you
I may be too young to know love
But I never felt so strongly about anyone
It may just be a crush
But I know it's not
As I said it before I'll say it again
I love you, I still love you and I will always love you.

Rolande Seudieu (12)
Riverston School

THE SKY

The sky with space above it,
Colours the earth within it,
It's grey, it's blue, it's orange too,
It rains from it.

The sea looks blue from it,
The earth looks white from it,
Stars shine bright from it,
The moon lights on it.

Thunder rolls from it,
Lightning strikes from it,
Storms rage from it,
Leaves swirl up to it.

Aeroplanes fly above it,
Wars are fought in it,
People look up to it.

Strength is gained from it,
And power is never drained from it.

James Thomas (12)
Riverston School

ARE YOU FOR REAL?

Of all the boys
I've ever met,
You're the one
I won't forget

And if I die before
You do,
I'll go to heaven
And wait for you

I'll give the angels
Back their wings,
And risk the loss
Of everything

Just to prove my
Love is true . . .

Marialena Andreou (16)
Riverston School

THE BULLY

I ran away from the bully
As fast as I could go
But there was no hope, so I stopped
and let him beat me so

I ran into him again, silly me
Scared, I ran away but he ran after me
I looked up, he looked down
And hit me to the ground

Next day I saw him again
I said to myself I will not run away
He came to me looking for money
I said 'I have none so go, go away.'

A few days went by and I saw him again
Running away from a bigger boy
I ran after them to see what was happening
And I saw the bully being bullied.

James Allen-Thompson (13)
Riverston School

FLORENCE

Some of the shops smell like fresh ice-cream
Big cones, little cones,
Flavours supreme
Chocolate, vanilla and coffee beans
These are the flavours I taste in my dreams.

A sun drenched piazza
Echoes with sound
Mopeds, bicycles, chatting all round
German, French, English, Chinese
A real language soup topped with Italian cheese.

The gold painted ceiling of San Lorenzo dome
Around this magnificence the people roam
Along to the bridge of Ponte Vecchio
Lined with street vendors,
Selling shoes, bags and clothes
Streets lined with copies of Italian art
Can be seen from the tour of a horse and cart.

The smell of leather
The stall holders shout
The market is buzzing
Bargain hunters are out
Refreshment time
Pizza and wine
Cappuccinos all round
Enjoy the street mime.

A last lazy wonder
Through the Florentine streets
A breathtaking vista
Around the corner greets
A marble clad vision
A cathedral divine
Gold leaf on paintings
From renaissance time.

Maryanne Carlin (13)
Riverston School

BULLYING

Bullies are like lions ready
to hunt their prey.
Bullies are fierce and will
keep on going if no one can
stop them.
To the bully victims are like
scorny little runts.
The victims are scared of
what is going to happen to them.
Bullying is like a sort of treachery.
The victim is humiliated
in front of people at school.
Bullying is like a diabolical plan
to hurt others.
Bullies, are like hated things in
society. Beware or be scared.

Simeon Brown (13)
Riverston School

I SHALL RETURN

I shall return of course I will
With strength and hope and awesome pride.
To fight against my daily stride
Which I began a long time ago.
I shall not rest
Until I get the best.
I see no reason why gunpowder treason
Should have a go at all.
For God who loves us
Would not forsake us
And let us go astray.

I shall return of course I will
To do my father's will.
Which I will be proud of
And say it aloud
For everyone to hear.
To ease my mind
Of long years of pain,
For I shall soon be praised.

Henrietta Taylor (14)
Riverston School

ANGER

It's like a bull
It stamps on anyone in its way
It feels like you have just been smacked with a bat
It's like a vacuum cleaner
Consuming anything pure and good.

This is anger.

Victor Alaike (11)
Riverston School

HARVEST

The night is dark,
The night is cold,
Fishermen on the deck
Dreaming of bed.
From where I stand
I listen to men shouting.
Round and round
The strong smell of fish
Here and there.
All you see of the fishermen
Is the oilskin and sou'wester
In the beam of light from the lighthouse.
They have a job to do.
Catch the fish for harvest day.
Now the sun is up
And they will go home
To bed!

Michael Brooks (13)
Riverston School

HEAVEN

I looked up at the sky
Thinking about heavens glory
And its pure light shining bright as the sun
This world is like an ocean of sins and evil.

Oh God please vanquish all those that cause this
And let this world live in peace with you
Around your burning gold throne surrounded with angels
We can live happily without crime
We just need pure goodness.

Bhavik Upadhyay (13)
Riverston School

Castaway On An Island

My eyes awake to see a bright sight,
Sand almost white, deep blue sky.
I stand up and think what a beautiful place,
If only I could share it with you!
It's days like these which make you happy,
I love the sun because everyone seems merry!

My friends awake at the break of a new day,
What a beautiful day,
We may be stranded, but we don't care,
The sunshine makes us want to survive through the day!
We look for food, but all we find are coconuts which we have eaten for
the past week!

Once the dilemma of breakfast is over,
Activities for the day is what we need,
I jump in the sea which looks so clean, the fishes you can see,
It feels like a fish tank with water so clean, I can see fish and lots of
coral reef.

I walk around to find some peace,
Then I sit and think to myself I may be happy, but what about my
family?
My lonely daughter how I miss her so, she's only two,
I've missed the best years of her life, soon she'll be grown,
Her long brown hair, her favourite toys
I hope she's safe and warm,
Mummy's coming it won't take long just be strong,
I'm there in your heart!

As night draws near, so does a tear,
A tear of sadness, a tear of joy, a tear for all those I love
As I lay my head thoughts start to whirl,
Round and round in my head they go!
Tomorrow's the start of a new day,
Different feelings and different thoughts,
A message in a bottle, I will write!

Natasha Clarke (14)
Riverston School

BULLYING POEM

Like a roaring lion he comes
Ready to kill, steal and destroy.
One look from his wicked red eyes,
Will see you have nightmares
To haunt you for life.

You go home bruised and battered
The world is like nothing,
It's just you and the bully
Everywhere you go
You can't escape.

But then there is a light at
The end of the tunnel,
'Childline' helps you
The bully no longer looks
At you with red eyes
The world is all right.

Akinsola Akinbolagun (13)
Riverston School

GOING, GOING, *GONE!*

There was a cloud of strangeness, a persistent eerieness,
Hovering in the sunless atmosphere,
A ghoul lingering, ever so slowly, across the sky's suspense
The spookiness of the silence, so supernatural, so intense,
As a mystical and unusual presence.
'Run! Run!' screamed the mind of a young boy,
His face stained with blood
His hurrying pigeon steps,
Quickened in pursuit of harder, heavier thuds.
He had only gone to fetch his ball,
Not at all prepared for this unexpected scare
But now, was found on this living odyssey
Indeed, a true and mortal nightmare!
The heart beats of his booming adrenaline
Echo the pursuing plunges of his predator,
This extraterrestrial
Ready to kill!
Approaching from behind, coming closer
and closer,
and closer,
Until . . .
The young boy could not escape any more,
Could no longer resist the craze of this mad chase
Running, perplexed, challenged by lazy legs
In this endless maze
Fear and fright replacing the white
With a grimace on his red, dripping face.
He had strived to keep alive but unfortunately,
What was supposed to be his prize
Turned out to be an award of awful cries!
Felled on deaf ears, triggering increased fears.
He had run for so long,
But now, was clenched in the hand of the evil one
Ready to attack -
Johnny had been caught, and unfortunately,
Wasn't coming back

Where he is now, is where his future lies
Everyone remains mystified by
The dropped dagger glistening evilly in the red sunlight
All that is known, is that he travelled with trauma on the track
Terror at his back
Thrown into a terrible trap.
All alone, all by himself
Where could little Johnny possibly be?
Harassed by the haunt of a perpetual jaunt
On the course of an unexplained odyssey.

Seke Bangudu (16)
St Francis Xavier Sixth Form College

GUESS WHO

They whisper,
At times they hiss.
In the night, the whole generation shimmers.
What a beautiful sight!
Oh and when the moonlight outshines
The slithery-like beauty
Never scared of the gloom.
They listen silently
But talks they don't
They keep all your secrets
All . . . in their hearts.
Their silence,
Their peaceful quietness
Does pierce the air.
Restores a lost soul
And brings to rest a troubled
And hurt heart.
That is what they create.
Guess who?

Brenda Osieyo (16)
St Francis Xavier Sixth Form College

Purifications From Above

God created man and woman
One flesh, one body, one heart and one soul
The stars and light created by God, God's might
Six days of creation, he rested on the seventh.
Darkness into light, angels' white chariot floating in the sky
He taught us to use our faith and to be blind to lies and deceit.
Christ gave us life for all his children of might,
For each person in God's eyes is special no matter what race or kind.
We must seek his knowledge and wisdom learning to purify our hearts.
We must also learn to respect ourselves
Then we can respect who so ever may come our way.
We must not judge others by physical appearance
But search to see what lies within.
Friendship and love is also important,
You have friends who have betrayed your heart
Leaving you through difficult times within your life,
Then your friends who will give their all
Guiding you through trials and tribulations.
We were all young once
Making mistakes and moving forwards from them.
Our soul requires love,
Learning to love you first
Is more important than loving someone else.
Our passion in life is to achieve our dreams and aspirations conquering the world,
There may be struggles and obstacles in the way
But never give up because determination is one of the keys to life.
The soul is the greatest creation of all
Making each individual special and unique
Hand to a glove he created the stars above
So let's spread the love that our God gave to us.

Francessca Haffner (16)
St Francis Xavier Sixth Form College

WHAT IF...

A wise man once said:
'Live each minute as though it were your last -
For what if tomorrow never comes?'

To know is to understand . . .
To learn is the beginning of knowing.

When acts are carried out in the name of civilisation
Yet executed with such barbarity;
How many tools is a man armed with
That he is gratified to possess,
Yet implores to never use?

The mind's landscape is a place of no return -
A graveyard of shattered but unyielding thoughts.

Fallen angels will sometimes mount up their wings
Like keen-eyed eagles
And somehow find their way home,
Forgetting the residue of unspoken bitter words
Reserved for the faceless assailant.

In a perfect world,
Broken dreams are but scars on the horizon.
At daybreak, only God knows what tomorrow beholds
The panorama of 'what ifs' and 'maybes' and 'just in cases . . . '

Tariro Masukume (17)
St Francis Xavier Sixth Form College

DROWNING IN MY SURVIVAL
(STILL I RISE PART 2)

Wake up and sip the liquor as I touch the ground with my lifeless feet,
Early morning woken up by Tupac's sinister heart skipping beat.
Blood on my tears as I pop out of my vein,
Suicidal emotions have been warped around my brain.
My poetry is my ambition, my life, philosophy and tradition,
My 17 year journey through hell was an exploiting expedition.
I'm determined to live out my dream as I drop the ancient scriptures in a poetic manifest,
A rhythmic mariner off on a global conquest.
I rap to my deceased peeps and to uphold God as he embraces,
I hang on the cross with the nails embedding through my palms with invisible traces.
Close my eyes, and feel my heavy head bop to the intoxicating beat,
Lie down, release my stress - search many souls and remember that I haven't got enough money to allow myself to eat.
Knife fights and gats bite - tricks lie and then cops turn a blind eye to let the youth to die, all equal to a painful trance,
To survive in this world for another minute - and I'll tell you I haven't got one single chance.
My soul's locked down - ain't no time for surviving.
Sick of having to look over my shoulder - can't knock the hustle but I'm better off dying.
I pray for change, but I am what I am - a street survivor whose cerebral cortex expands when times get hard,
I rap for listeners and women - blunt heads, hustlers, gangsters, and killers - whether on the streets, deceased or behind bars.
Pay attention to my raps cos my raps are real,
Stimulate your cerebellum to make you feel my thrill.

My avenged poetry is defiant as I scream with every throaty syllable that any day could be your last in the jungle,
If you stumble on your journey you could get murdered on the tumble.
So I drink the delusional rum to release my paranoid worries from my world's devastation,
Now I speak to you through a revolt theorem to corrupt your mind with anticipation.
My lyrics on life hit the world like a comet - a street dweller that's created his own fashion,
Gripping the nation in a tight hold, as you understand that my rhyme power is passion.
In my vision - I've realised that to be heard, that you need to have a high status or a high salary,
I've risen my life from living on a dark street clouded with misery and pain as I stand and become a liturgy prophecy.
Now breathless - instead of saying f*** tomorrow, hope to survive another 24 and that my family and friends can follow.
To enclose with me - I send respect, peace and one love. Rest in peace Devon, as you watch on from the heavens above.

'Revolt', Sacha Jason (17)
St Francis Xavier Sixth Form College

FUTURE VOICES

They told me to write a poem, so I have written them a poem.
They told me to work hard and get good GCSEs and not stray
                                        from the path they chose for me.
I have written a poem, a poem they won't like,
A poem showing not the me they created but . . .
The me I am.

They told me to dress smartly and told me not to dye my hair,
They told me who I was, and I believed them.
They told me what I would achieve and why I wasn't good enough
                                            for this or that,
And they told me how to live my life and . . .
Now I've answered back.

Frances White (15)
Sydenham High School

A MILLENNIUM POEM

M usic to dance to all night.
I   ncredible things in the Millennium Dome.
L ovely, coloured fireworks.
L aughter and joy.
E ndless amounts of noise.
N on-stop happiness.
N ot working yet wheel.
I   n all the squashed streets.
U nbelievable millennium bridge.
M illennium really marked its spot.

Lucy Kiernan (13)
Sydenham High School

THE SEAWEED BATH

Two mermaids play in the bath,
They giggle as the seaweed slips through their fingers.
One dreams of jumping and diving
In and out of the water;
The other of friends with mermaid tails
And the palace under the sea.
Hand in hand the two swim,
Sisters as never before,
Towards their place of paradise
In the salt water.
They fulfil their dreams,
Then swim back to reality.
The water drains away,
Nothing remains of their brief escapade,
Except a slimy tinted green residue
And happy child-like memories.

Theadora Foster (14)
Sydenham High School

SEMBLANCE OF A SMILE

Eyes of emerald green,
Twinkling in the moonlight.
Dusty sable hair,
Dropping seductively over your brow.
Your smile so shy,
Your touch so gentle.
But underneath lies a shattered soul,
An empty heart,
An inner war,
Hidden by a smile and the twinkle of an eye.

Angelique Forrester (14)
Sydenham High School

PUSSY CAT

Pussy cat, pussy cat
Where are you?
Look there he is, cosy and warm.

Pussy cat, pussy cat
Time for dinner
Not too much or he will get fat.

Pussy cat, pussy cat
Oh please come home
I'll hug you till you are lovely and warm.

Pussy cat, pussy cat
I have a surprise for you
It's a nice new ball of string for you to undo.

Samantha Eniola Pereira (12)
Sydenham High School

WHO AM I?

Every morning I give a loud neigh,
Just as long as I get my hay.
Who am I?
I gallop around the fields and jump the logs,
Taking care not to sink deep into the bogs.
Who am I?
I have a silky, long, bushy mane
My rider on my back holding me tightly by the rein.
Who am I?
My neck is long and my hooves are shiny.
My tail is bristly and my body is tiny.
Who am I?

Natasha Mitchell (11)
Sydenham High School

WHEN THE CLOCK STRUCK TWELVE

Some people said the world would end,
Others thought they were round the bend.

Why do we think of these things,
We should be happy for what life brings.

We just had to wait and see,
What the 21st century would bring for our destiny.

We watched the clock with our family,
Forgetting about Christmas and the tree.

The last few seconds suddenly came,
But if something went wrong, who would be to blame?

It was all over and the world hadn't ended,
There it stood still looking splendid.

Aysem Hashim (13)
Sydenham High School

THE CLASSROOM

Pencils scribbling away on paper.
The clatter of pens dropping to the smooth floor.
Yelling, shouting and then a commanding voice, now silence.
Laughing.
Arms waving the air.
Books and stationary spread over tables.
Bags, bulging with books, hiding the floor.
A bell rings. Chairs, tables pushed aside.
Books thrown in bags. Feet stomp.

Silence.

Leila Sharif (12)
Sydenham High School

The Fox

Slyly, carefully, he places his paws precisely down.
His deadly eyes pierce straight to the heart like a thousand daggers.
His ears pricked,
He listens for the slightest footfall.
Through his curved nostrils he smells the scent of danger,
The scent of a hunter,
A deadly scent,
The scent of death.

Swift and silent are his fast footfalls,
Along he races carefully, precisely still.
He hears behind the heavy clumsy footfalls of the hunter.
As his speed increases, his soft orange fur is blown gently back.
He turns,
Hides behind a tree
The clumsy hunter passes.
As danger disappears,
He again becomes the hunter,
Not the hunted.

Katie Mountain (11)
Sydenham High School

The Cat

When it wakes
It arches its back.
Its claws sharpen,
And it pounces.

It jumps so delicately off the fence,
And lands on all four of its paws.
Its claws sharpen
And it pounces.

Her green eyes get thinner,
As she searches the garden.
Its claws sharpen
And it pounces.

Its claws sharpen
And it pounces,
It arches its back,
And starts looking for its next prey.

Louisa McLellan (11)
Sydenham High School

A PLECO'S JOB'S NEVER DONE!

I slither, I slide
I glide along the stones
I hide behind a log
Waiting for when it's time to do a job
The algae that sits on the side
Waits for me to awaken
I glide up to it, before you know it, it's gone.

When night appears
I open my glowing eyes
I swim swiftly to the top
And I come back down
I suck the side of the tank
With my hover-like mouth
I cut the algae that grows on the side
By the time you awake
I'll be back behind my log
Waiting for another night on the tiles.

Charlotte Oram (11)
Sydenham High School

THE FAMOUS NIGHT

The famous night of new beginnings, expectations.
The night to make resolutions.
The time to start afresh.
Caught in a giant wave of hype, anticipating the 12th chime, they wait
They watch.
Breathless.
What will happen?
1, 2, 3
An explosion, an end to our planet?
4, 5, 6
A massive volcano?
7, 8, 9
The sky opening?
10, 11
12.

Some fireworks.
Some cheering.
People go home and a tramp lies in the gutter, trying to keep warm,
So easily forgotten.

Julia Charteris (14)
Sydenham High School

MILLENNIUM 2000

They build a bridge
It starts to wobble,
They build Dome
It brings nothing but trouble.

The colourful fireworks
Light up the sky
There's a magnificent view
From the London Eye.

We've changed to pavements
From cobbled streets,
But we still have the parliament
Where the MPs meet.

Now we have a
Multicultural society,
Unlike before when
We suffered from anxiety.

Elizabeth Afolabi (13)
Sydenham High School

DOLPHIN

I swim through the sea like every day,
It's peaceful as can be, I swim elegantly,
I look at my family,
I have a lot to learn.

Today the poachers are back,
My mum tells me to stay away,
But I couldn't feel curious
Although I was warned.

We ran as quick as air
A flock of dolphins called us
The dolphins showed me to attack,
Every single fish was eaten
Run, I heard that must mean.

Humans there, here I was scared
What shall I do?

Chloë McCarthy (11)
Sydenham High School

The Architects

Pyramids pointing up to the sky
Built bravely, brick by brick by sweating slaves.

Mysterious and magical, wrapped in white and gold,
The Taj Mahal - an eastern beauty.

Precariously, the tower leans at Pisa,
Beautifully built, a landmark of the nation.

Canterbury, Winchester, Salisbury, and Gloucester,
The cathedrals show the craft and skill of the builders.

Sydney opera house, swan-shaped
Sings proudly by the harbour.

And then in Greenwich . . .
The Dome!

Alice Lindsay (12)
Sydenham High School

Something To Celebrate

Thousands throng into Greenwich, what a sight!
To celebrate 2000 years on one great night.

The Queen, the Duke, Tony and Cherie Blair,
And anyone who's anyone is there!

Fireworks and music, all to bring good cheer,
And just to celebrate another year!

Champagne and caviar and so much to eat!
Meanwhile the homeless still sleeping on the streets.

Elizabeth Lindsay (12)
Sydenham High School

2000

Earth,
A place without time or meaning,
A land where the sun means light
And the moon is just a torch in the dark.
Caveman,
Resorts to primitive ways,
Eats live animals,
The word 'time' serves no purpose.
Sun,
An instrument used for telling the time
Day,
Night,
Moon,
Earth,
A place with time,
A place with early people, late people,
People with watches, people with clocks.

2000, the time has come.

Beatrice Butler-Bowdon (14)
Sydenham High School

THE MILLENNIUM WHEEL

Does a hamster feel the same?
When round its wheel it goes all day.
But ours is slow, oh so very slow.
Although coming down is quite a shame.
It's huge, it's vast, and it's seen for miles.
A new attraction, for different styles.
Our beautiful city is seen all around
And everyone comes off covered in smiles.

Annie Broadbent (14)
Sydenham High School

Fallen

The time has come where I become detached
And learn of new beginnings,
As the darkness falls I lose all strength,
And what is left of me, is mocked by my rivals.
The time has come.

As the colour drifts from my outer skin
The inner life becomes a distant memory.
My fate draws ever closer as others take to their deaths,
The illuminous sun loses power and leaves me in despair,
All that is left of me is my memories;
Memories of children, children running round and round.
The time has come.

My inner sanctum cries out for understanding.
All that is left is a gust of wind and I am fallen;
Fallen from my home, my family.
My crisp outer shell leaves me vulnerable,
And all that is left is my dignity to keep me alive.

Nicola Graham (14)
Sydenham High School

The Leaving Of The Elephant And Elephant's Eyes

Every morning I wake up,
Lying awake, looking up at the sky,
Every night I go to sleep,
Peering up and wondering why,
Hearing my friends sleeping tonight,
And seeing them twinkle in the starlight,
Now or never I must leave,
Tomorrow will be the time to heave.

Eating breakfast,
You're giving us lunch,
Eating dinner, a delicious brunch,
So now I've got to say goodbye, are you okay?
Oh please don't cry . . .

Duriyen Mehmet (11)
Sydenham High School

THE KEEPSAFE NECKLACE

I stare at the necklace,
As it twirls round and round,
Never to be worn by her again, but I'll keep it.

I devour the smell,
Hungrily wanting more,
The stale perfume has lost its charm,
I cannot make it return,
No one can.

I examine its every detail,
The diamonds glow like the stars in the blackest night,
The silver, new as ever,
The chain, sleak and long, curling round,
My hand like a snake.

I place it in its box,
As black as black can be,
I close it,
I've trapped the necklace
Never to escape.

She will never see me again,
She is gone,
As I am now in spirit.

Jemma Jackson (14)
Sydenham High School

MYSELF AND ME

I hate it,
I have to live with it day and night,
But I can't keep away.

As I look in, I smile,
But my nose stretches and my teeth are sharp.
I look down and curse myself,
Let me hide in shame.
I must leave dignified but thankless,
Thinking of famine and feeling so vulgar.

I can feel myself falling, falling,
Slipping away,
There is nothing to hold onto.
Darkness is closing around me and I feel myself reaching out.
As I touch the box, icy, cold and sharp,
All I can see are the consequences.

Hide me,
Oh God, let this swallow me,
Then I could stay there and be happy.
But give me strength,
In there, there is no exit for hours.
It is round,
A vicious circle which echoes my every move.

It is the appalling noise that frustrates me most,
It makes me feel so light but I could sink at any minute.
It's so common,
I am no longer immune.

Rachel Harvey (14)
Sydenham High School

ARE THERE ANY ANSWERS?

It was never meant to happen,
It just occurred all of a sudden,
Without warning,
It felt as though the world had come to an end,
It felt as though shutters had been clamped down around us,
No light was to be seen,
It was dark, dark.

No one knew about it,
No one was ready for it,
Was this a punishment?
Was this a curse?

Am I wrong in saying that this was unfair?
Because this really was unfair.
Am I wrong in saying this was cruel?
This really was cruel.

Maybe this was meant to happen,
Maybe his time was up,
Was this destiny?
But gone,
Gone without a goodbye,
Just leaving us,
Leaving us hurt, confused and disturbed.

I ask God why?
Why this has happened,
And I wait, am still waiting,
But never is there an answer.
Is there a God?

Sheena Ganatra (14)
Sydenham High School

MY SANCTUARY

I looked up, awed,
I have decided this is a special place,
And this is my special place,
And this is my tree.

As the tree stands towering over me,
I feel safe,
Under its strong branches,
And large, shiny, pale green leaves.

Sitting under my tree,
In the warm, dappled light,
Filtering through the branches,
I can sit and dream.

I think back to the childhood I never had,
Swinging through the branches,
Climbing, clambering,
Happy in my childhood nativity.

But this never happened,
Not to me anyway
My childhood was not blissful,
Far from it.

But now,
I can look to my tree,
Strong and permanent,
For comfort.

So as I sit in this secluded place,
My place,
Shrouded by the green, green ivy,
And lying on the green, green grass.

I talk to you, my tree,
I ask you to look after me,
Always,
Always.

And I know,
My tree will still be there,
Standing tall and strong,
My sanctuary.

Forever.

Charlotte Head (14)
Sydenham High School

TODAY

Today I went into hiding,
I don't know what to do,
I'm scared and extremely frightened,
I'm sure you would be too.

Today I went into hiding,
I don't know what to say
So I talk to my pet cat, while he urges me to play.

Today I went into hiding,
I don't know what to think,
It's cold and dark; I'm lonely,
I'm afraid to even blink.
If I move they may hear me and soon break down the door
Then I will be more frightened than I've ever been before.

Tana Forte (13)
Sydenham High School

SACRIFICE

The leaves were ruby-red, amber and emerald green,
The sky was clear and blue.
Gentle breaths lay on the air,
Zephyr whispered softly.
A rustle from a mountain of dead, damp leaves made me stop
                                        and turn to look.

From its warm, dark haven, an adder emerged,
Smoothly slithered, graceful across my path,
His mottled green scales glinting in the golden sunshine.
I was awed by his beauty, his agility.
He snaked past the leaves that littered the path, and I,
                                  fascinated, followed.

He swept his long, sleek body past fallen red berries,
Wound round thick tree stumps,
And in the shadow of the roots of a gnarled horse chestnut tree,
He stopped.

He lifted his head,
And looked around him with jewel eyes
And licked the frosty air with his tongue,
He seemed to glare at me,
As if to ask why I was watching him, but also to say he didn't mind,
So I stepped back into the shadows,
And turned into an oak tree, whose branches reached high up to the heavens.

The snake drew himself back down,
And gazed intently on a patch of dewy green grass.
A tiny brown mouse scurried out,
Its black, beady eyes glancing around,
Its ears twitching nervously,
And it looked up,
Straight into the glistening eyes of its killer.

A gasp escaped my lips.
The inhumanity, the brutality,
Of the mouse devoured whole,
The petrified squeal
Of the petrified creature.

The scene of death
Would not leave my mind,
Although I pressed it away,
Again and again.

The snake licked his lips,
Satisfied.
He paused, and drew himself into a midnight black opening
                                                        under a root.

I let go of my leaves and ran.

Annabel Head (14)
Sydenham High School

DON'T DARREN

Don't pick your nose Darren,
And please don't sniff.
Don't tread the mud Darren,
All through the hall.
Don't stuff tissue Darren,
Down the plug hole.
Just don't do these things Darren,
Just try to be good.
For once in your life Darren,
Please show me you could.

Laura Jones (13)
Sydenham High School

Giving Way To The Light

I can't figure it out.
Is darkness growing?
Creeping up on the sunset's golden glow.
Reaching out its mysterious black limbs,
And overtaking the rich oranges with its morbid black hue.
Too strong for light to defend its territory.

Maybe darkness is a magician of the sky,
And casts a spell on the sun.
Soothingly sending it into a deep sleep,
Carefully easing the sun's rays out of the sky,
And leaving it content with its midsummer night's dream.

So now the night is here.
Darkness majestically rules over its kingdom in the sky.
But where is everybody now?
Soon darkness' feeling of isolation has grown
Stronger than its foolish pride.
Darkness breaks down and once again,
Gives way to the light.

Sophie Hughes (14)
Sydenham High School

Behind Closed Doors

I am trapped in this dark box
With nowhere to turn or hide.
The lioness roars, I scream and shout
I am sent to the corner.

I wait for the lion to return
To unlock the chains tied around me
Holding me tight
Unable to escape.

I fear for my life
I'm scared of death.
I'm too young to die,
If only the lion would return.

I want him to be present
With me forever
But like my dad,
The lion never returns.

Emma Louise Frempong-Manso (14)
Sydenham High School

THE KING OF THE JUNGLE

I wouldn't like it at all to be a lion in a zoo,
With people standing there to see the lion things I do,
I'd rather be in a jungle land beneath a jungle tree,
With only jungle animals to stand and look at me,
I roam about the jungle all day,
Every minute I'm growing grey,
Everybody knows me,
As well, as well can be,
Some animals say that I'm so lazy,
But I know that they're so crazy,
I know I roar so loud,
That is why I'm proud,
I love to eat,
Lots and lots of meat,
The cry of hungry beasts,
The lion at his feasts,
Animals are scared,
I know that they're afraid.

Devisha Patel (11)
Sydenham High School

GRIEF

Motionless sat the mourners
as the clouds drew across the sky,
pear teardrops, augmenting in a father's eye.
She is no more.

Greyness sweeps the family,
drowning the entity of black.
A mother's sobs,
enveloped,
in an air of despair.
She is no more.
Eyes pool of pain.
Pale faces,
twisted by emotion.
She is no more.

Silently left the mourners
as the rain tumbled from the sky.
Pear teardrops augmenting in a lover's eye.
He sits there,
in grief,
alone.

Agatha Knowles (13)
Sydenham High School

THE MILLENNIUM? - 30 SEPTEMBER 1970

In the millennium, we're all going to fly,
Fly into space, with red and green eyes.
We'll live on Mars, what fun that will be,
No more swimming in the sea.

Will we have work? Will we have play?
Will children get a say?
How many times will we change our clothes?
What will we weigh? Nobody knows.

Party all day, party all night,
The neighbours will certainly get a fright.
I'll have a robot to clean my room,
Maybe school will be on the moon.

But the millennium is so far away,
Perhaps I'm wrong and it will cause dismay.
Will it be announced by a big, loud gong,
No matter, I probably won't even live that long!

Chloé Brown (14)
Sydenham High School

UNITED

Somehow everything for one moment seemed good,
No one seemed to grieve for lost loved ones,
Everyone was joined, all daughters and sons.
I wonder if the animals can perceive,
The unbelievable legacy the millennium does leave
And understand what the commotion was all about.
Was it some milestone the whole world felt?

One night the birds did not rule supreme.
The sky, magical, like a child's dream.
The stars envious, their crowns stolen,
Robbed by showers of colour which had fallen.

Music played from instruments loud and clear,
So deafening millions of people could hear.

People laughing, cheering, holding hands.
As they danced and cheered along with musical bands.
Excitement in every child's heart like it was their birthday.
'Happy Millennium!' people did say.

Sarah Baumann (14)
Sydenham High School

THE BIG NIGHT

The big night, everyone was excited
Crowds were forming all over London.
This is what people had been waiting for,
This was the new beginning.
There were millions of parties and many celebrations,
Lights and fireworks too.
The Dome was opened on the night and expectations were high.
Then everything was in place and the big countdown began!

10, 9, 8, 7, 6, 5, 4, 3, 2, 1!
Happy New Year!

Then that was it. The fireworks fizzled out,
The river never went up in flames
And crowds started to disperse.
It was already over and all that money wasted:
The Dome, the Wheel and the BBC's coverage all cost millions
And for what,
Only one year!

Katie Wardle (13)
Sydenham High School

2000AD

It all began with Jesus,
Who is a history of time.
So 2000 years have flown by,
We celebrate his birth, life and death.

1000 years ago, the first millennium,
Were people happy or scared
Of the end of the world,
But we will never know.

So the millennium has come and gone,
But what have we learnt.
Well, we know what happened,
We know 'The River of Fire' never burnt.

George Harrington (12)
Sydenham High School

MILLENNIUM POEM

Millennium eve.
How long we have waited
To see the turning of a century.
People wait, sparklers at hand.

As we wait for our millennium party,
The seasons are changing so slowly.
Our last year in the nineteen nineties,
Planning our eve slowly in stages.

Excitement is in the air,
As we stand on Westminster Bridge.
Honking horns and laughter are all
Around in the atmosphere.

Times went slowest that night,
After all the months of waiting.
Finally the clock struck twelve,
It was the new millennium.

A few fireworks and cheers.
Fifteen minutes later we all went home.
It was the anticlimax of the year.

Claire Brockliss (15)
Sydenham High School

THE ANTI-CLIMAX

Lots of people visited the Dome,
Others, like me, stayed at home.
Some people watched fireworks on telly,
While others worried about filling their bellies.

Some people thought that aliens would come,
Most people thought that was dumb.
Others thought the world would end,
I think they were going round the bend.

Finally the last few seconds arrived,
And to the twentieth century I waved goodbye.
Fireworks went off, crackers were pulled,
But that doesn't mean that I was fooled.

To me the millennium was just another day,
But people might think of it in a different way.
They might think it's a time to remember,
But what's the difference with next December.

Sorry I sound like a crashing bore,
But there are plenty of things I'd like to do more.

Jennifer Lock (13)
Sydenham High School

TIGER

T he only thing I think about is hunting my prey.
I creep across the jungle floor and hope to see a deer!
G ently the grass tickles me as I prowl across the ground.
E agerly I chase the brown distant dot.
R unning as fast as lightning speed . . .
   I caught my prey.

Fleur Nieddu (11)
Sydenham High School

The Everlasting Candle

The age has come
As we wait and wait
For the time when eternity ends.

When you close your eyes
Imagine the heavens
Covered with stars
Illuminating the sky.

We gather round
And watch
A flicker of light
Dancing before the naked eye.

Through the years it remains
Waiting as each day passes
Silent, yet still
For the dawn of a new age.

Only seconds to go
When we know the end is nigh
You watch the wax
Drip slowly down.

As the wick grows smaller
And the clock ticks away
Now is the time
To extinguish the flame.

There is no more
As I stand on the edge of the world
The Millennium has arrived.

Seraphina Evans (14)
Sydenham High School

WHAT IS THE PASSING OF TIME?

Nothing lasts forever,
Things fade away
Things fade . . .
Time takes over.

First the sun is shining,
And the flowers are blooming.
Soon they will lose their petals,
That settle on the ground.

One minute you're running on the pitch,
Then the next minute,
You're watching . . .
With your stick.

One day you're cradling
Your baby,
And the next day
You're kissing your grandchild.

One month your face is
As smooth as silk,
And the next month
It is as rigid as a crushed paper bag.

This is the passing of time.

Adelina Adjei (15)
Sydenham High School

EXCUSES

I missed the bus; I was going to be late,
I would get in trouble, which I really hate
You should not be late, the teacher would say
But she did not say that when I was late yesterday.

My alarm clock broke, I did not wake,
I had hurt my back, it really did ache,
I ran out of the house without my kit,
So at PE the teacher had a fit.

My dog ate my homework; I had to get it out,
He bit off my arm and then I had to shout,
After chasing him lots I retrieved my arm,
But I am afraid my homework came to great harm.

My mum was supposed to take me to school,
She totally forgot, what a very big fool,
I ran for the bus, but when I got there,
The bus drove off without a care.

You have been late all this week, this will not do,
You will have a detention and a letter home too,
I hope your parents teach you how to behave,
But I keep all those letters hidden tight in a cave.

Harriet Bothwell (13)
Sydenham High School

The Beach

Deserted and hidden
Behind a mountain high.
The only thing that knows about it
Is the deep blue sky.
So quiet, so calm, so peaceful
It all seems like a dream.
The place is still untouched
No humans have ever been.
The water is so clear
So lush, so cool, so deep.
Small sea creatures swim about
Beneath the ocean reef.
The sand, so soft, so warm
Heated by the sun.
Everything is so perfect
My beach, the only one.

Hayley Hawkins (14)
Sydenham High School

The Green Man

The green man's at the window,
The green man's at the door,
The green man's in the attic,
He's coming back for more.

The green man has a sparkle
In his twinkle eye,
I see the green man flying
Through the midnight sky.

The green man is resting
In his favourite tree,
When tomorrow morning comes
He'll get rid of me.

Nathalie Clough (12)
The Froebel School

BOREDOM

The bleak smell of home,
The embracing warmth
Lit with one small lamp,
Held together with one last thread,
One hopeful hand outstretched and a tear.
Yellow and messy, in the corner lay
The canned life, blaring and changing.
On the sofa lay the mass boredom
Of non-existence,
Warm and full of desperation and love,
But mixed with hatred and anger,
Sitting there, fixed on the blare.
But he was comfortable with the scene.
Him, spread out on the cushions,
Relaxed and wide open,
Glued to his seat yet hopeful to be released.

Gabby Laurent (15)
The Froebel School

MY HOUSE

When I was younger
I left my house
I threw away the key.
I dream of one day
Coming home to my house (number 4)
With all the rainbow birds singing,
All the flowers bursting up from the ground
Like a sea of jewels.
One day.
One day I'll come back
And my cat will be lying on the
Comforting grass under the sun
My favourite tree will be there
In my front yard, with its special leaves
Green, orange and red
One day.
One day I'll come back and my mint plant
Will smell of mint ice-cream,
We had it all the time.
I'll come back and my blossom tree
Will be giving off the sweetest smell ever,
A smell I will remember.
One day I'll come back
I know I will.

Erika Bacon (12)
The Froebel School

My Happiness, My Sadness

Scorching sun beats down on my face
Luscious, soothing
The big drink
Picking up the pace I go
Through thick or thin
Through fire and snow.
Thud, there's the punch
Poor Billy Blue
Brrrriiiing
There goes the bell
Time for lunch
He's left swimming in tears
Boo hoo!
Tangled blacks, browns, greens
Twisted oranges, blues, the best I've seen.
Blood!
The cry of the wild
Sense of danger
Drip, drop goes the rain
Death of the wise, wistful crane.
A thunderstorm
Lashes at the envious sky
The animals weep
And as the sun sets
The wise crane sleeps
As a new era is born.

Jade Wick (11)
Walworth School

MY LIKES AND DISLIKES

I like WWF,
It's real cool.
My favourite is the Rock
Too Cool too.
I like Pokémon
My favourite is Charizard.

I don't like peas,
Mash,
Snakes or spiders.
I like rough and tough football
But not boring, dull football.

I like life,
It's really wonderful.
I like all the plants and trees
I like all the maths and history we do in school
But I don't like boring ICT.

I like sports a lot,
I like South Park a lot
I don't like Winnie the Pooh.

Michael John (11)
Walworth School

FRIGHTENING NIGHT

I'm in my bed trying to get to sleep,
I pull the covers down and have a peep,
Because something is moving, it's starting to creep,
I'm very frightened, I'll never get to sleep.

It's on my bed moving closer to me,
My eyes are wide open but I cannot see,
It licked my face, what on earth is that?
A furry little monster,
No, it's my cat.

Good night.

Emma-Jayne Maflin (12)
Walworth School

MY LIKES AND DISLIKES

I hate bullies
They make school life hell
They make people hate school
Because they have been bullied.

I like my mum and dad
They take care of me
They buy stuff for me.

I like Christmas
You get presents
You eat turkey.

I like food
It's tasty
It smells good.

I love birthdays
You eat cake
You get a party bag.

I like holidays
You go on a coach
You go on the rides.

Omotayo Kukuspecial (11)
Walworth School

Autumn Poem

Leaves, leaves falling down,
Leaves, leaves turning brown
Autumn is here, autumn is here
Then next comes harvest here.
Here come heavy clouds, then it rains
And the raindrops fill the drains.
Here comes thunder, wind and lightning
It is really, really frightening.
The grey skies now turning black
What is worse than that?
Autumn is here, autumn is here
Then next comes harvest here.

John Olanipekun (12)
Walworth School

Colours

As pink as a porky pig,
As purple as a dressing gown,
As indigo as a magical fig,
As blue as the sky-high sky,
As green as a juicy apple,
As yellow as the sun that can fly,
As orange as a burning flame,
The colour red that can tame,
As gold as a gold, shimmering ring,
As silver as a shining star,
When all the colours start to sing,
The more colours it will start to bring,
A picture of who you are.

Sophie Morley (12)
Walworth School

WHAT DOES SORRY MEAN?

To me sorry is a word,
To you sorry can be heard,

Sorry, a word that can
Blow across the sky,

Sorry a phrase that
May mean nothing to you and I,

You can just say sorry
And not mean it,

You can be the sorry one
And believe it,

Sorry, can be a moving bird
Sorry can be a 50/50 word.

Nicola Hold (12)
Walworth School

A POEM ABOUT THINGS I LIKE

Dogs can be big,
Dogs can be small,
But I don't care at all.
Boxing is a contact sport,
When you box you have a lot of support.
Football is the best if you have Cole forget the rest,
Snow is white and pure, snow fights are the best,
You normally get in a mess,
Simpsons, South Park are cartoons,
Bart is bad,
Kenny dies and Cartman's always eating pies,
Rockets *zooming* through the air.

Morgan Schofield (11)
Walworth School

My Likes And Dislikes

I like flowers when they are in bloom
I run away from bees, I hide in my room.

I love the moon when it shines at night
But ghosts and ghouls give me a fright.

The World Wrestling Federation is bad
But the Tweenies are so sad.

My family is the best
But cabbage I detest.

With my friends I like to play
But my enemies don't get the time of day.

Football is my favourite sport
Hockey I dislike and can't be taught.

Life is beautiful, we all agree
Death is something no one wants to see.

I love my trainers I think they are neat
Can't stand my shoes though, they hurt my feet.

Charlie Brightwell (11)
Walworth School

What Makes Life Enjoyable?

I like South Park
Simpsons and other joys
Playing games with cuddly toys.

Playing football in the parks
Listening to music in the dark.

These are some things that I like
But there are always some dislikes.

My dislikes sometimes differ
My most disliked are hot, roast dinners.

Punching, kicking, slapping, teasing
Bullying is most displeasing.

Sarah Coote (12)
Walworth School

LIKES AND DISLIKES

They are sweet and are any shape or size
Animals
I love them.

You find them in any library up on the shelf
Books
I like them.

They lend a hearing ear, they comfort you when you're sad
Friends
I'm glad I have them.

Long and twisty, it gets you in a mess
Spaghetti
I love it.

They come in different shapes and sizes with one thing in common
Bullies
I hate them.

They crawl about all over you and try to suck your blood
Bugs and spiders
They freak me out.

They sneak about grabbing what they can
Thieves
They should be locked up.

Julia Sykes (11)
Walworth School

My Likes And Dislikes

It is nutritious
It keeps us alive
Eating
I love it.

It hurts people's minds
And you are not a true friend
Gossipers
I hate them.

It keeps me happy
It makes me look funny
Laughing
I love it.

It gets people into trouble
It makes people cry
Liars
I hate them.

They are dirty
They smell
Pigs
I hate them.

They advise us
They don't make us feel lonely
Friends
I love them.

It teaches us about the future
We learn from it
Reading
I like it.

Bukola Ogunjimi (11)
Walworth School

SEIZING THE DAY

I like to watch horror movies
I like to touch furry animals
They are so sweet
They can be neat.

I like swimming
I like to watch telly
I like to eat jelly
Whilst I'm watching telly.

I like to dance
I like to sing
It does me really good
You do some exercise.

I hate it when my mum mashes up my mash
It really does my brain in.

I hate it when people start to argue
I really don't like it
I just walk away.

I hate shouters
It makes me jump
I don't like to jump.

I don't like watching football
It causes arguments
And they get the hump.

Chelsea Kelly (11)
Walworth School

My Punishment

As I remember my crime I'm sent away
And I feel I've been walking for days and days and days.
As I enter the room that you hear screams and shouts
Where people receive their punishment.

I see the dragon known as *The Head*
As he breathes his fiery breath
I just know what's going to happen
I'm going to receive my punishment.

He looks down at me with his bright red eyes
Just staring, staring, staring and waiting, waiting, waiting.
'What is your come, oh silly, stupid one?'
He said with a voice sounding like a billion crowds.

As I tell him my crime he says
'Oh why, why, why' you have to receive your punishment
Now I scream
After years and years I finally got out of that nightmare
I had received my punishment!

Susan Wain (12)
Westwood High School for Girls

My Mum

My mum is like a teddy bear
Warm and cuddly, there when you need her the most
My mum is like a volcano exploding at the slightest thing
My mum is like a flower, sweet-smelling and short.
My mum is like a chocolate bar, hard on the outside, soft on the inside
My mum is like my best friend you can tell her anything, any time
But best of all she's my mummy.

Loredana Geoghegan (13)
Westwood High School for Girls

My Treasure Trunk

Come and share my treasure trunk
Come and see what I have.
Come and look at my photos.
Come and share my memories.
Come and see my family,
Come and see my pets.
Come and share my
Gift of my life.

Come and share my treasure trunk
Come and see what I have.
Come and look at my photos.
Come and share my funny jokes,
Come and laugh at my jokes.
Come and stroke my pets.
Come and share my love.
Come and laugh at me.
Come and share my things
That I have in my treasure trunk.

Nicole Iesi (12)
Westwood High School for Girls

Things That Are Treasure

T is for *Treasure* the kind you never lose
R is for *Ruby* that shines so bright
E is for *Emerald* that sparkling piece that hangs round your neck
A is for *Amber* that is never forgotten
S is for *Sapphire* the one we all desire
U is for *Unisex* for both women and men
R is for *Rings* that last forever
E is for *Everything* that sparkles.

Nikki Harman (12)
Westwood High School for Girls

ALPHABET POEM

A utumn is when the leaves fall on the ground
B lack skies all around
C louds scattered all around in the air
D uring Christmas and New Year
E verything looks nice this time of the year
F orgetting the rest of the year
G rey skies scare me
H igh up in the sky
I cy sky falls sadly
J ust before the storm
K ites are blowing in the sky
L et's see how high
M ums are muttering madly
N ans mutter loudly
O h what a great sight
P eople out and about all night
Q uiet has come around
R est and peace, there is no sound
S urprise, suprise
T here's another day ahead
U p gets everybody
V ery much to do
W inter is coming
X mas is nearly here
Y es it's Christmas
Z ipperdedo! Presents are here.

Kylie Wood (12)
Westwood High School for Girls

WHAT IS A REAL TREASURE?

I found the real treasure,
I really found it.
It is so wonderful,
A heart filled with love!

I found the real treasure,
Which is a gift of life.
I don't want to lose it,
It's very precious to me.

I found the real treasure,
A treasure of friendship,
A treasure that gives life.
It's not that expensive,
It's a sea of free love!

I found the real treasure,
A treasure I love.
It's part of my family,
Which is my mum!

I found the real treasure,
She shares her love.
She rains her love,
The storm of love.

I found the real treasure,
I really found it.
It is so wonderful,
A heart filled with love.

Arooj Ahmed (12)
Westwood High School for Girls

COMING TO ENGLAND

My heart is like a silver star
Spilling silver dust everywhere.

My heart is like a humming bird
Singing sweet melodies in every note.

My heart is like a magic flower
Swishing happiness to and fro.

My heart is like a golden sea
Splashing the silver rocks.

My heart is like a white dove
Because I'm coming to England.

Jodianne Griffiths (12)
Westwood High School for Girls

BOOK OF MEMORIES

I still remember the book of memories,
It reminds me of the past.
It's a gift from God
Which wouldn't last.
There were happy moments and sad
It was full of photos,
Like how my life and my brother's and sister's life began,
It was like going back in time,
It's very precious and valuable
I will never forget the book of memories.

Fahmida Mossabbir (12)
Westwood High School for Girls

TREASURE

Treasure can be evil
Treasure can be precious
Treasure can be love
Treasure can be expensive
Treasure can be junk
Treasure can be an enemy
Treasure can be waste
Treasure can be anything you want it to be
Most people don't know what treasure really means
But to me it means a lot
My family and my friend are my treasure
So come and share my treasures.

Anntoinette Ussher (13)
Westwood High School for Girls

MEMORY BOX

Come and share my memory box
It holds all my treasures
Over the past few years
Photos and lockets
Love and peace
A lifetime of all my memories
Photos of friends and family
Of hen nights, stag nights and anniversaries
Photos of weddings and parties
Sad and happy moments
That I will keep
Until my time has met with me.

Opal Plummer (13)
Westwood High School for Girls

Clumsy

'Late again,' my teacher said
'I'm sorry but my dog jumped on my leg.
I've now got a bruise from my thigh to my knee
And then my sister came and walloped me.'
'Yeah right' said my class
And I moved really fast
Over to the door
On the way there
I tripped over a chair
My teacher screamed 'No get back over here'
Then, I don't know why, there came a tear in my eye
My teacher said 'Go and sit down'
And I did with a frown.
I opened my book
And my friend shouted 'Look'
I went all red
And my teacher said
'Don't worry it's only a blot.'
Then the bell went
And I bent
Over to get my bags from under the table
I walked home in sorrow
'Perhaps' I thought
'It'll be a better day tomorrow!'

Amy Heard (11)
Westwood High School for Girls

MY TREASURE

My first birthday present,
From my best gran ever,
It's a hand-made blanket.

My name in red,
With silky thread,
And bright flowers,
Around the edge.

I love my blanket,
I still love it so much,
I feel safe when,
I used to snuggle up . . .

It was my play mat,
My magic carpet,
My crazy house,
My best loyal dressing gown!

I still have it,
And always will,
Because it's my *treasure*
And I will keep it forever,
And ever . . .

Hayat El-Daoud (12)
Westwood High School for Girls

WHAT IS THE PURPOSE OF TIME?

I think as I sit on my bed,
What is the purpose of time?
I hands on the clock go around and around
And Big Ben always strikes on the hour,
But still, what is the purpose of time?

Some days go quickly
Some days go slowly,
Others just seem to fade away
But still all around the world the clocks are ticking,
What is the purpose of time?

Time goes quickly when you are enjoying yourself,
When you're on holiday, playing in the sand.
But, it goes slowly when you are really bored
When you're in your worst class in school.

This is all associated with time
But I still wonder
What is the purpose of time?

Justine Bristow (12)
Westwood High School for Girls

ONE OF MY TREASURES

I've got a treasure
I want you to hear
It's about my gran
She's like my best friend
Sometimes she'll scream and shout
But afterwards she'll be alright
Most of the time she's alright
And on Friday's we'll stay out late.

Keisha Bristol (12)
Westwood High School for Girls

COME BACK

You're the ache in my salt fish
You're the sugar in my tea
You're the mango tree in the garden
And the birds that sing for me.

You're the little children laughing
That play out day and night
You're a little dotted star
That is shining bold and bright.

But once again I'm crying
Waiting for you to come home
I see your face in the window
And two seconds it's gone.
You left me here alone
Leaving me to grieve,
I wish you'd come back
So you can comfort me.

Adriana Crooks (12)
Westwood High School for Girls

TREASURE

Come and share my treasure trunk
And you'll be my very first hunk.
Even though sad days pass
We'll make it last.
You can share my gold and silver
With joy and happiness forever.
When we break up
My mouth will be shut
And I will start to dream of my family.

Charlotte Nash (12)
Westwood High School for Girls

Treasure Chest

Come and share my treasure chest,
Where your eyes will shine so bright
It's not just jewels
        money
                and diamonds
But memories
        love and life.
Thinking of the things you love
May not be the things you trust.
So dig down deep into your soul
Maybe love and peace will emerge
I see blue skies and summer days
With words of happiness through the air
I see myself in still-life pictures
Which bought my smile right up to my ears
So glad it wasn't an ugly task
So I didn't have to dig too fast
To find that love and happiness
Just inside that treasure chest remembering
It's not just jewels
        money
                and diamonds
But memories
        love and life.

Claudine Parr (13)
Westwood High School for Girls

My Treasure

My treasure was my little cat
She was my faithful friend,
A fluffy, little tabby
I loved her to the end.

She died when she was seventeen
I cried for her for days
And I will always remember
Her cute and funny ways.

Jenny Demmen (13)
Westwood High School for Girls

IT POEM

I   nformation Technology is amazing
N othing is better than that
F ont can be changed
O r even the colour that
R ange the size you want
M aterialistic font
A ttention to the computer
T yping can begin
I   n the computer there are microchips
O n clarissworks you go
N othing can beat a computer

T yping day and night
E verything on the Internet
C hat rooms for you and me
H appy people and sad people
N either you or me can work out where they go
O n the printer things can be printed
L atest technology
O ut of Internet
G oing computer crazy
Y ou can do all of this you know.

Laura Mitchell (11)
Westwood High School for Girls

TREASURE

Here are my treasures
That I've packed away
They're more than just jewels.

Memories are one of them,
Photos are another,
My family are the most important.

We've had laughs,
They've made me cry
They are who I love and cherish
I will always remember them even till the day I die.

My treasures are going back now
To keep them safe and dry
I hope you enjoyed sharing them with me.

Do you have any treasures?

Maria Tough (12)
Westwood High School for Girls

TEACHER'S POEM

Let the children in our care
Clean their shoes and brush their hair.
Come to school on time - and neat
Blow their nose and wipe their feet.
Tell the children not to eat in class
Or run in the hall, walk like they are small.
Let them show some self control
Let them slow down, let them stroll.
Let the children walk not run like they are mad
With a six foot mother or a seven foot dad.

Monique Baker (12)
Westwood High School for Girls

The Line Of Life

My treasure is my life
And I'll live it to the max
But my life does give me strife
I sometimes wish I could have time back.

It's never been regretted
That my life is how it is
My life's a never-ending line
With lots of knotted times
But my family will help me through these knots
And help me through this time.

Everything happens for a reason
And that reason is much loved
Like me to my family
And my family to me.

When I'm grown and big and bold
And look back on this and laugh
I'll say to my children 'Harda har'!
And help them walk the line.

Simone Byer (12)
Westwood High School for Girls

Schools

S   chools are supposed to educate people
C   hildren don't really care
H   oping that one day they're going to become rich
O   h no! That's not fair
O   nly the smartest people get far
L   ots of girls do their own thing
S   o sorry! I can't go on, I've got to drive my car.

Jade Ashman (11)
Westwood High School for Girls

My Treasure Trunk

Come and share my treasure trunk
I'll tell you what's in it.

It's full of dreams and secrets
That need to be told
So listen up because here I go.

I hope I become
An engineer of computers
So I'll have lots of money to spend.

I love my family
Because they show me love
That no one else shows.

I have baby pictures
That no one else has seen.

So don't go round telling everyone
My dreams and secrets
Let them read it *here*.

Sumayya Choudhury (11)
Westwood High School for Girls

Olympics

O is for open-minded when you're on the track
L is for long jump crashing in the sand
Y is for yelling at the end of the match.
M is for medals gold, silver and bronze
P is for people rooting for their teams
I is for injuries that can kill the competitors dreams
C is for commentators *Oh, what a goal!*
S is for Sydney where the Olympics were held.

Rhea Currie (11)
Westwood High School for Girls

TREASURE

Treasure, treasure, treasure
I keep all my things as a treasure
Come and share my lovely treasure
With all the hopes and love which you won't see ever.

Treasure, treasure, treasure
I keep all my dreams in my mind as treasure
Treasure, treasure, treasure
I have a dream of diamonds, but I can only imagine
But cannot see, is it real or not, just tell me.

Treasure, treasure, treasure
I like reading, singing, dancing
I want to keep them as a treasure
Forever and ever.

Ameena Salik (13)
Westwood High School for Girls

TREASURE BOX

Come and have a look at my treasure box
It's full of fun and joy
Come and see my treasure box
Come and have a look.

It's full of goodies for all
Come and have a look
It's full of memories
Love and friends and families
Gold and glitter and a touch of glamour
Come and have a look at my treasure box.

Louise Johnson (12)
Westwood High School for Girls

THE END OF THE BEGINNING

The movement and sound of living things
The light and colour of movement
Moving slowly around the earth
Swirling round and round then
One dark and lifeless day
The movement and sound was lost
Light and colour were smeared
Into lifeless dirt
Evolution started here!
This is where the world got in gear
But out of the dirt a thing did crawl
A scuttling thing that creeps and crawls
Upon this creature new life will form
Another kingdom will be born.

Gemma Agard (13)
Westwood High School for Girls

COME AND SHARE MY TREASURE CHEST

'Come and share my treasure chest'
It's taken years to fill
It's full of photos of pets, family and friends.

'Come and share my treasure chest'
Toys and games are inside
Birthday and Christmas cards since I was one.

'Come and share my treasure chest'
It's full of memories
They're priceless to me, to you it's old junk
But to me there's a lifetime of memories.

Hannah Stevens (12)
Westwood High School for Girls

First Gift

My first gift was a green tortoise,
Cuddly and all soft,
Now it is a multi-coloured piece of junk.

My friends' teddies are all modern
They see mine and turn in disgust.

To me my teddy is gorgeous
To me my teddy is fine
To me my teddy is wonderful
You see my teddy is *mine*!

You see my teddy is my soul mate
He is perfect for me
Me and my teddy are meant to be.

Elizabeth McAuslan (12)
Westwood High School for Girls

Treasure

When I lay in bed at night
I think of all my treasures
Family, friends
And the things that mean so much to me.
I think about my life so far
And all the treasures given
Like teddy bears and blankets
But most of all love.

Joanne Machin (13)
Westwood High School for Girls

My Treasure Chest

Come and see my treasure chest
It's full of lovely gold
With pictures of me and pictures of you
The one I love the most.

Come and see my treasure chest
It's full of lovely things
They bring back loving memories
I think I am gonna weep.

It's got pictures of me and my teddy bear
I got her when I was born
And when I could talk I named her
'Snowflake Marvin Mour'.

Her nose has been chewed up
Her sack has come off her back
I still have Snowflake
She sits on my chair
And listens to my problems
And that is why I love Snowflake.

Tyenicha Hewitt (12)
Westwood High School for Girls

Treasure Box

Come and share
My treasure box
With peace and passion
For my family.

Come and share
My treasure box
With fun and joy
For everyone
Gold and silver lockets too.

Come and share
My treasure box
With memorable photos
Of lots of events
That we do.

Come and share
My treasure box
With shared moments
Birthdays and Christmas
Weddings we will remember.

Josephine Osei-Nyarko (13)
Westwood High School for Girls

MY TREASURE

My family mean everything to me
Like no one could ever know
I love them very dearly
And I would never share them at all.

I think of good and bad memories
But some make me depressed
Instead I think of my mum and dad
And all of the good times we have had.

My favourite toy is my teddy bear
Who I have had since the day I was born
I would never give her to anyone
Not anyone at all.

This is the end of my poem
So now you know a bit about me
Of how much I mean to my family
And how much my family mean to me!

Terriejane Snell (12)
Westwood High School for Girls

THE GIFT OF ME...

Open the door and see my treasure
I had a gift to give
See what it is . . .

They looked
They smiled
They touched
They loved
They hugged
They hoped she was well
She cried, they sang and comforted her
They wanted her to be part of them
They wanted to give her the world
They wanted to give her a future
Have you guessed who *she* was
It was *me!*

Lucy Adams (12)
Westwood High School for Girls

MY LITTLE BABY BROTHER

My little baby brother was born on a rainy day
Is like a sunshine to me.
My little baby brother sweet and tiny
Means the most to me.
My little baby brother cute and cuddly
Brings the most happiness to me.
My little baby brother weepy and naughty
Still is the most precious one to me.
My little baby one however he be
Will always mean the world to me.

Razia Jeerooburkhan (13)
Westwood High School for Girls

TREASURE TRUNK

Share my treasures with me now
I've packed away the memories.

I've looked at the photographs
They have made me remember
All the things I have done.

Every day they make me cry,
I'll always remember them till I die.

Now close your eyes and bow your head
And think of those poor people who are dead.

I hoped you've enjoyed yourself
I'd better go, but remember about what I've said
And every night bow your head.

Natalie Parbodee (12)
Westwood High School for Girls

COME AND SHARE MY TREASURE TRUNK

Come and share my treasure trunk
I'll tell you what it contains.
It has all my memories of when I was little
Also when my nan died I treasure that forever.
I love my family with all my heart
It will stay like that forever.
I remember when I was little
I got a princess dress, it was pink and sparkly
My family is very precious to me.

Kirsty Dowling (12)
Westwood High School for Girls

CATS!

Cats walk around with pride,
Showing their cats' eyes,
They like their fish, they do,
Some cats are playful, they're the ones who are nice,
But some cats kill mice.
Cats are fluffy or sometimes bold,
But rarely ever scares,
So if a cat comes up to you,
What do you start to think?
Whether the cat's happy or whether the cat's sad,
But I'll tell you one thing,
When there's a crime,
No cats are there to be scared!

Sarah Benham (11)
Westwood High School for Girls

MY POEM

Come and share my treasure trunk
Come and see what you could share with me.

You can see my happy memories
And share my sad ones too.

Have a day with me, even spare some time
For me to share my treasure trunk.

Come and see what you could share with me.

Michelle Scripps (13)
Westwood High School for Girls

THE LOVE

Love
Love, love makes my fun go round
Love is kind
Love is in the air
Love makes my life worth living
Love is nice
Love is at home
Love is in school, in class
Love is everywhere
Love is my life
Love is my teachers in a teacher sort of way
I love McDonald's, McDonald's is the best
I will sing along and try my very best.

Sara Widdowson (11)
Westwood High School for Girls

MY TREASURE TRUNK

Come and share my treasure trunk,
I'll show you all my treasure.
I'll share it with you
I promise I will.

It's a big brown box with my treasure in
I'm not lying.

I've got a secret too
To share with you
It's all about treasure trunk.

Come and share my treasure trunk
I'll show you all my treasure.

Farah Parekh (11)
Westwood High School for Girls

MY NAN

Twinkle, twinkle little star
Even though you're so far
I wish that you could be here
Oh I love you nanny dear.

I think of you in my sleep
Even when I'm counting sheep
Sometimes I even cry
I sing myself a lullaby
Oh I love you nanny dear.

I just wish you were here
I love you so much
I even pray that I could
See you for one more day.

Kylie Evans (12)
Westwood High School for Girls

HEAVEN

There it is
White and clear
It soothes away any fear.

Reassuring, loving and kind,
It cools my busy, crazy mind.

There it is
Warm and true
Welcoming me and you.

Tacy Ram (12)
Westwood High School for Girls

My Necklace

I have a treasure, come and see
It's gold, silver and precious to me
The gold symbolises everlasting love
The silver symbolises a peaceful dove.

It is very round,
It weighs a pound,
It is quite long,
It plays a song.

I'll always remember
The 15th of September
When I got my necklace
From a shop called Texas.

Charlotte Edwards (12)
Westwood High School for Girls

Absent Minded

A cloud of blue flakes fluttered
Into quick silver beads like rain
The figure slowly formed out of air curled and crinkled
Fading like bright smoke
The shadow was stuck against the air
By some magician's glue
A husky voice spoke
'I'm going to be lonely.'

Hina Khwaja (11)
Westwood High School for Girls

OPEN UP YOUR HEART

I saw it
I've seen it before,
Don't ask me what,
You know what,
Your treasure chest.

Not the one full of jewels,
But the one full of love.

Your treasure wants to be shared,
Come and share your treasure with me.

Your heart,
Our memories,
Are the only things,
They keep my heart going,
Beat, beat, beat, beat,
Day after day after day.

Love to see
Love to hear
Love to smell
Only you.
And I love to love you so.

Open up your heart,
Like a treasure chest,
So warm,
So full of good,
And let me love you,
Just a little more.

Charlene Gogognon (13)
Westwood High School for Girls

SPIDERS

In a dark, gloomy and damp place,
Two spiders lurk.
Looking, looking
For a safe place to build their thin and shiny webs.

They're crawling about
As nightfall comes
Everything is silent
But in the distance,
Two spiders crawl about.

Dawn is near
But they don't stop.
Their eight legs are walking fast,
As they keep on searching,
Searching and searching.

They are tired
But they can now stop looking.
They have found the right place
As they walk about
Busy weaving their webs
Nightfall comes
Yet again.

They wait in their webs,
Something is on their webs.
They quickly pounce on the unfortunate thing.

Their dinner has been served,
So now they can rest.
Still they are waiting,
Waiting, waiting.

Diana Monteiro (11)
Westwood High School for Girls

MY TREASURE

My towel is my treasure,
It's tiny and so small,
I've had it for 12 long years,
And my name is embroidered on.

My story book is my treasure,
It's really small and sweet,
It's from a girl called Emma,
And she loved for me to have it.

My rabbit suit is my treasure,
It's tiny and it's small,
It's soft and cuddly,
With ears and floppy feet.

My favourite treasure is my love,
With my mum and dad,
And my two brothers,
No matter what happens, I love them all the same.

Emma McDowell (12)
Westwood High School for Girls

MY TED

I love my Ted
I call him Fred
I tuck him in bed
Close to my head.

In the night
When I get a fright
I will hold him tight
So monsters don't bite.

Shikiera Betts (11)
Westwood High School for Girls

WHAT A DAY

When I get home
At one, two or three
It's normally on a Thursday
To see Auntie Patsy

Coming from my auntie's
Bordered than bored
I look down and notice
My trouser had torn

As I stroll up the stairs
Nothing's on my mind
Then I remember give diary to Miss
But I haven't got it signed

In my room
Music blasting in my head
Mum said 'Turn that down'
I think I'll turn it up instead.

Cherrowne McPherson (11)
Westwood High School for Girls

MY JOY

It's a sunny day
And I feel so fine
Flowers and roses
Are going to be mine

Walking and jogging
Nothing on my mind
Waiting for somebody
To give me a good time.

Nicole Ramsay (12)
Westwood High School for Girls

My Brothers

I have two brothers,
Who think they are in a bother.
They love to scream and shout,
They also love to run about.
They spray water at me,
And then I cannot see.
They like to fight all the time,
When they like to act out as Mr Mime.
They do not have time to do their homework,
While they are trying to open the bottle with a cork.
He gets told off by his mum,
Then she starts to hit him on his bum.
And then they go
Wa! Wa! Wa!

Aisha Abid (12)
Westwood High School for Girls

Mmm... Tastes Good!

Liquorice, Starburst all the lot,
Cola, Fanta love the pop!
Haribo is just for me,
7-Up is for a treat.

Fish and chips have a nice smell,
Fried chicken has a succulent smell.
Raspberry ripple with Vienetta,
I love the smell of Hubba Bubba.

Chew, chew ... bubble ... pop!
I love the taste of lollipops!

Jemma Haynes (11)
Westwood High School for Girls

Sports

Do you do basketball?
Do you do ice skating?
Do you do baseball?
Do you do roller-blading?

Can you do high jumps?
Can you do netball?
Can you do low jumps?
Can you do football?

There's lots of sports
You can do
They are in your thoughts
So let them come true.

Zainab Dawodu (11)
Westwood High School for Girls

Rain Drip-Drops

Saying go away rain,
Don't come again rain,
Drip-drop, drip-drop,
Drip-drop, drip-drop.

Drip-dropping on my windows
Drip-drop, drip-drop,
I say bin those drip-drops
Again . . . and again.
Drip-drop, drip-drop.

Natalie Preen (12)
Westwood High School for Girls

THE SUN

I'm sitting in the garden
Under the beautiful pleasant sun
While I'm doing my homework
In the garden, oh it's so much fun

I can hear birds singing
Merrily up in the trees
Buzzing sounds around the flowers
Of busy bumblebees

Kids playing, cats laying
On the greeny grass
Large and beautiful butterflies
Fluttering their wings go past
Smokes from the coal smells of the barbecue
Makes my stomach rumble
Ants gather around
My plate of apple crumble

Sun is so good
Sun is so fun
It makes a better world for everyone.

Zeenat Malik (11)
Westwood High School for Girls

AUTUMN

Orange and yellow leaves,
Fall from the trees
Fall into the river
And sail into the sea.

Children come out
With woolly hats
Scarves and anoraks.

At the end of the day
They jump into bed
Ready to wake up
For another day to play.

Michelle Wain (11)
Westwood High School for Girls

WHAT'S THAT IN THE KITCHEN?

It is midnight
The back door is open
I need a cup of water
I have my torch.

I slowly walk downstairs
I am scared of the dark
I am a few steps
Away from the kitchen.

What's that in the kitchen?
I think it's eating away
It's big and hairy
With two beady eyes.

It might be eating the cupboard
It might be eating the washing machine
Or the sink,
Or it might eat me.

I'm walking closer
Aah! It jumps
I reach for my torch.

What's that in the kitchen?
It's my dog!

Niroshine Sureshkumar (11)
Westwood High School for Girls

What's Love?

Is love just a word that comes and goes?
Is love a feeling that grows and grows?
Is it mesmerised?
Is it hypnotised?
Is it a next heartbeat we hold with all our pride?
Is it a mixed-up feeling? I can't decide.
Is it something hated?
Is it located?
Is it as pure as a dove?
So can somebody tell me
What's love?

Justine Tulloch (13)
Westwood High School for Girls

Love And Hate

Love and hate is down to fate
No one can pick or choose
It's down to Cupid
If you choose it you'll lose it.
So just remember these rules:
Remember love goes both ways
It's not just a passing phase
And hate is not down to fate
It's deep within your own control.

Justine Agbowu (14)
Westwood High School for Girls

MY HAMSTER STUMPY

I have a hamster called Stumpy
He is black as night and just a bit white.
One day he escaped into the night to give my sister a fright
Then all of a sudden there was a scream
Which came from my sister's bedroom
A large crowd gathered around the bedroom
Then my sister said 'There's something on the floor.'
In came my dad and said 'What a bunch of scaredy-cats.'
On his knees he lifted the pillow and opened a grey box
And inside was my hamster Stumpy chewing a sock.

Tina Bigley (11)
Westwood High School for Girls

BOY COUSINS

Boy cousins, boy cousins are such a pest
But I guess they're for the best.

Boy cousins, boy cousins always protect me when I'm in trouble
They're always there on the double.

Boy cousins, boy cousins do really love me
But it doesn't show when they're around me.

Boy cousins, boy cousins how I love my boy cousins.

Tenika Chin (13)
Westwood High School for Girls

THE LAST BARK

I heard the cry, as the brakes screeched stop,
I saw a blur of a white mop.

I heard a last bark, then all went quiet,
As I looked out the door I sure saw a sight.

I touched its soft fur and felt its warm paw,
Then tried to bring it back to life once more.

The poor creature lay still resting on its head,
Then after a moment, I realised it was dead.

Angela Hazell (12)
Westwood High School for Girls

MY MUM

I love my mum with all my heart
In my life my mum plays the most fabulous part.
She buys me things and cooks my tea,
That is why she is my mummy.
When I've been naughty and very bad
She starts to go very mad.
Then I say I'm sorry Mum
Then she says come on, come.
I go over and she gives me a cuddle and a kiss
And don't be naughty again my little miss.

Danielle Harris (11)
Westwood High School for Girls

Guess What I Am?

I am big and hard
My outer body is green.
When you cut me
I am red inside with pipes.
I am very juicy and mouth-watering.
What am I?

I am shaped in a curve
I have a yellow coat
From the top of my head you peel me.
I am on a tree until somebody picks me off.
What am I?

Precious Ihuomah (11)
Westwood High School for Girls

Distant Dreams

When I'm asleep my dream comes true
Then pops in my mind a wonderful fairground
Nearby in the distance I see the sunset
Shining down on the ocean
I also see and hear waves rippling
Against the crunchy, soft sand
There goes the carousel round and round
First my eyes start to open
And I give a great yawn
So I wish that my dreams will come true.

Lauren Andrews (11)
Westwood High School for Girls

CHILDREN

It's a sunny morning,
A beautiful day,
All the kids go out to play.
They play in the park,
They play in the streets,
All until it's time to eat.

After lunch they go back to play,
Down in the woods is where they will stay.
Playing like mad,
Having fun one and all,
Getting all messy,
They don't care at all.

Laura Einecker (12)
Westwood High School for Girls

NETBALL

I enjoy playing netball
Even though I'm not very tall
My best position is goal defence
To me netball makes a lot of sense
I have to mark wing attack
And then throw the ball to someone in my team
Sometimes my team flows like a stream
I love netball very much and after practice
I have packed lunch.

Sabrina Wholas (12)
Westwood High School for Girls

Abandoned

I was sitting in my room
I felt cold and lonely
I felt like I was being pushed aside
Left out.
Sadly I thought nobody cared
I had been forgotten about
Tears rolled down my face
As I got frightened
I felt like I was being isolated
I was being *abandoned!*

Ahzaraieha Harvey (11)
Westwood High School for Girls

Love

I   hate you

L   eave me alone
O   ff you go
V   ery big mistake I did
E   very time I see you, you make me smile

Y   ou're very close to me
O   fficially the best
U   nderstanding better than the rest.

Manisha Sharma (12)
Westwood High School for Girls

THE BULLY

The bully
The bully
So cold and dark
I look into his eyes
And see a coward

The bully
The bully
So tall, frightening
So big and broad

The bully
The bully
You don't frighten me
You don't scare me
You just make me laugh

The bully
The bully
I will beat you
I am stronger than you
All you are is a big coward.

Vikki Heath (12)
Westwood High School for Girls

LOVE

Love is a feeling
Love can be felt
Love is so precious
It can make your heart melt
A touch, a kiss, a hug, a kiss
Love is always made of this.

Tara Forde-Wildman (11)
Westwood High School for Girls

Something

Where something?
Who something?
How something?
What!
Tell me what you mean
You're getting me hot.

What is it?
Where is it?
Please tell me
You told everyone else
Even snotty-nosed Lee!

If you don't tell me
You'll annoy me a lot.
Where something?
Who something?
How something?
What!

Louise Thompson (12)
Westwood High School for Girls

My Fruit Poem

I'm nice not too round,
I'm sweet but get cut down,
I've got pips inside of me,
I'm full of juice inside,
But I'm not that wide on the outside.

Crystal Lindsay (11)
Westwood High School for Girls

FOUR SEASONS

The flowers were blooming,
the bees were buzzing,
the birds were chirping.
It was spring.

The sun was shining,
the beaches were bursting,
the drinks were flowing.
It was summer.

The leaves were falling,
the birds were migrating,
the animals were hibernating.
It was autumn.

The snow was falling,
the skies were greying
the preparations for Christmas were beginning.
It was winter.

Fozia Haroon Karim (13)
Westwood High School for Girls

SECRET LOVER

She has a secret lover
He's fast, wicked as can be,
They make love in the night
And make everybody see
You may think it's an awful sight,
But to see such delight
Is pretty as can be.

Kim Carter (12)
Westwood High School for Girls

UNDYING LOVE

When you said we had to part
I'll tell you now you broke my heart.

As I walked back from the street
A single tear fell down my cheek.

As I walked back on home
I really thought that you would phone.

I walked into the kitchen and picked up a knife
And decided then to take my life.

Into my wrist I began to tear
A drop of blood fell on the chair.

Then you shouted through the door
Can't we kiss and be friends once more.

But even with your loving charms
My heart stopped beating and I died in your arms.

Laura Panayides (13)
Westwood High School for Girls

WORM

Little worm wiggle wiggle
You make me and my sister giggle
You live in mud
You live in wet
But yet you never see the vet
You must be a very healthy worm
Wiggle wiggle wiggle squirm!

Nicola Claridge (13)
Westwood High School for Girls

GHOSTLY DOVE

What name do I give you,
when your face is so soft,
that of a white velvet rose.
Your eyes that are sharp brown,
of the eagle in paradise,
your lips, deep red,
of a tulip, so rich in its colour.
Your hair, a simple brown,
with a soft silken touch.

What do I say.
when your lips move,
yet you say nothing.
Your eyes close,
but you don't blink,
your breathing, moving,
but no sound.
You'r there, then you're not.
You move, yet I see,
there's no cast of a shadow.

I see, I speak, I say.

You are
soft, silken, sweet,
like a ghostly dove,
so elegant, in its style,
so different, in its view,
or . . .
Are you even that . . .

Are you even there . . . ?

Tasneem Haroon Karim (15)
Westwood High School for Girls

Animal A-Z

A ngry ants attack anxiously
B usy bees buzzy breezily
C lever cats climb carefully
D izzy duck dives deeply
E normous elephants exercise everywhere
F unny ferrets fall forwards
G iant gorillas growl grumpily
H appy hippos hop home
I cy iguanas in igloos
J ealous jaguars jumping
K haki kangaroos kick kettles
L azy lions leap leaves
M arvellous monkeys mop mansions
N aughty newts nip nastily
O range octopuses open oozily
P ink panthers pick plants
Q uincy quails quarrel quickly
R ed rabbits race round
S illy snakes slither slowly
T iny toads trop together
U gly unicorns undo umbrellas
V icious vultures vomit victims
W icked weasels weave webs
E xcellent foxes expect exercise
Y yellow yaks yell yes
Z any zebras zip zippers.

Sophie Hassel (12)
Westwood High School for Girls

SMILE

If you smile it will be worth your while.
I like to smile.
Your smile is like a ray of sunshine
Shining on me.

If you smile it will be worth your while.
You like to smile.
My smile is radiant
It lights up the whole of my face.

If you smile it will be worth your while.
We like to smile
Our smile lights up the whole room.

So if you smile you know it is worth your while.
So go on smile.

Sophie Rankin (12)
Westwood High School for Girls

THE RIDDLE

Do you know a riddle,
Like 'Hey Diddle Diddle',
Where the cat did play a fiddle,
Right in the middle of the street,
The street was so cold,
As the legend was foretold,
For when the press heard of this mess,
The poor little cat was sold.

Donna Stanley (14)
Westwood High School for Girls

BEST FRIEND

Best friend, best friend
Never broke up.
Best friend, best friend
Never fight.
Best friend, best friend
Never bully friend.
Best friend, best friend
Never leave each other.
Best friend, best friend
Stay happy.
Best friend, best friend.

Marium Bhatti (12)
Westwood High School for Girls

WHAT AM I?

I am bright yellow
I'm a shape of a moon
Peel off my skin I'll still be yellow
I taste very lovely and I'm very long
Soft when you peel off my skin
You'd love to eat me.
I begin with B
What am I?

Mariam Mehdi (11)
Westwood High School for Girls

FRUITY POEM

I feel a bit bumpy on the outside
But I am not on the inside.
My colour orange makes me so bright
But once you've eaten me I'm surely out of sight.
I feel a bit sticky but that's alright
But once you've eaten me it is really alright.
What am I?

Christina Murray (11)
Westwood High School for Girls

WHAT AM I?

I am long and curved,
The shape of the moon
Yellow-skinned, smooth.
Easy to peel.
Inside I'm creamy white.
Dots run down inside me.
What am I?

Kelly Goff (11)
Westwood High School for Girls

THE STREETS AT NIGHT!

The streets at night, give me a fright,
So lonely damp and cold
The stars shine bright, all through the night
The moon we can behold.

So silent, so still
I can't help to feel so lonely and scared inside.
A scary feeling that I know, the streets so long and wide.

Grace Coughlan (13)
Westwood High School for Girls

WHAT AM I?

I have a green coat.
Inside I wear a red shirt.
I am full of water, I am very juicy.
I give you wet hands and I am also sticky.
My name starts with the letter 'W'
What am I?

Pinar Mehmet (11)
Westwood High School for Girls

FRUIT POEM

I'm red on the outside
Orange in the middle
I'm nice and juicy
And tasty to eat.
You will be silly,
So just eat me and see.

What am I?

Natalie Papaspyrou (11)
Westwood High School for Girls

WHAT AM I?

I'm the jazziest fruit you'll ever see.
I'm very juicy and I weigh a lot.
You can only eat me if I'm ripe
You can't miss me.
I'm never out of sight
My body is round and prickly
And knife-like spikes grow from my head.
What am I?

Marsha Francis (11)
Westwood High School for Girls

WINTER DAYS

The windy cold days are back
Cold gushes of wind
Snow all over the floor
Santa Claus is back
All the kids are happy
A new year is here.
2000!

Sandy Lee (12)
Westwood High School for Girls

TIME

Time is what flows like water
Not caring who is left behind.
Bringing bad luck for some,
And leaving behind for others laughter.

Try to run ahead of time,
Or soon you could find yourself far behind.
No station, no stop comes in its way
So when you deserve it don't be declined.

Atiqa Khan (13)
Westwood High School for Girls

21ST CENTURY

Christmas is coming for the 2001 time,
2001 years have flown by,
Christmas is coming for the 2001 time,
Christmas, millennium, goodbye, goodbye.

21st century here we come,
Flying cars and everlasting gum.
Flats on Mars and unbreakable bars
And robots that can do every sum.

Rachel Irwin (13)
Westwood High School for Girls

FRUIT POEM

I'm small and sweet,
Good to eat
Green and purple
Easy to eat
Peel the skin
If you must
Bite me
Taste my sweet juice.
What am I?

Kirsty Aboagye (11)
Westwood High School for Girls

SEASONS OF THE YEAR

Spring is a time of bloom and blossom
Trees are blossoming
Flowers are awakening.
Our sun is more alive
And all things begin their lives.

Summer is a time of sea breeze and laughter
Everyone on their holidays
And children play in glory.
The sun sets late and rises very early.

Autumn is a time of amber colours and autumn fall
When night closes in
Beautiful leaves fall
To complete a wonderful layer of amber colours
Brown, red, orange and yellow to make a carpet.

Winter is a time of sweets and snow
As you walk out you feel the glow.
On Christmas Day children play.
You feel a warm rich feeling of all foods
That are for special occasions.

Jane Sammut (11)
Westwood High School for Girls

ALL ABOUT ME

My name is Grace
I have a lovely face.
I don't use too much toothpaste,
I like a race
With my friend called Ace
But I always trip over my shoelace!

Grace Mann (12)
Westwood High School for Girls